Bilka Baloh is a researcher and consultant for healthy and balanced nutrition, and therapist of Ayurveda, and a lecturer and mentor for therapeutic fasting. She helps people with a wide variety of imbalances in the body. Bilka devotes herself to hills, climbing, yoga, and meditation. She is a visionary and sets her goals high. Her life motto is never to give up! She says that life is a predetermined plan we were given at birth, and we cannot escape it. "However, we can partially change and improve the plan with a healthy way of life and ethically blameless behavior towards fellow human beings, animals, nature, and the entire creation. Work on personal development is healing wounds from the past and treatment simultaneously because all diseases originate from unresolved conflicts deeply rooted in our subconscious. The key we're all looking for is self-love."

If you want to know more about Bilka's work visit her website. https://bilkabaloh.si/en/

# Bilka Baloh

# FASTING EXPANDS CONSCIOUSNESS

## The Wisdom of Cellular Intelligence

AUSTIN MACAULEY PUBLISHERS™

LONDON • CAMBRIDGE • NEW YORK • SHARJAH

**Ordering Information**
Quantity sales: Special discounts are available on quantity purchases by corporations, associations, and others. For details, contact the publisher at the address below.

**Publisher's Cataloging-in-Publication data**
Baloh, Bilka
Fasting Expands Consciousness

ISBN 9798889101642 (Paperback)
ISBN 9798889101659 (ePub e-book)

Library of Congress Control Number: 2024904900

www.austinmacauley.com/us

First Published 2024
Austin Macauley Publishers LLC
40 Wall Street, 33rd Floor, Suite 3302
New York, NY 10005
USA

mail-usa@austinmacauley.com
+1 (646) 5125767

I dedicate this book to my mom and dad.

*O! never say that I was false of heart,*
*Though absence seemed my flame to qualify.*
*As easy might I from myself depart*
*As from my soul, which in thy breast doth lie:*
*That is my home of love; if I have ranged,*
*Like him that travels, I return again,*
*Just to the time, not with the time exchanged,*
*So that myself bring water for my stain.*
*Never believe, though in my nature reigned*
*All frailties that besiege all kinds of blood,*
*That it could so preposterously be stained,*
*To leave for nothing all thy sum of good;*
*For nothing this wide universe I call,*
*Save thou, my rose; in it thou art my all.*

William Shakespeare (1564–1616), English
playwright and writer, Sonnet 109[i]

First, I wanted to understand the disagreements that I
had had with my mother. It took me a long time to
know why my soul chose her as my biological mother.

When I realized that our souls chose our parents, I started researching my ancestors. I was given a fantastic genetic code and less beautiful karmic records. My transformation is still ongoing, but my mother and I have finally become friends and companions in this material world. We respect each other and no longer limit ourselves.

Dear Mother, I am grateful to you for all the lessons I needed to build my personality as a soul. Thank you for accompanying me on this thorny path, supporting me and never judging me.

I am also grateful to my father, who always encouraged me in my ambitious and avant-garde projects. Dear Father, you believed in me even though you often said that I'm an altruist who can't take care of myself and that you were a bad father. Until I realized that it was your pain, not mine, I didn't understand. Today I know and accept you exactly as you are. When you want to accept something, you are in the role of a victim, but when you understand a certain thing, it is a matter of consciousness. This sequence is saving and healing at the same time.

[i]https://www.poetryfoundation.org/poems/50301/sonnet-109-o-never-say-that-i-was-false-of-heart

Thanks for the book's creation go to some of my colleagues who believed and still believe in the benefits of fasting and my work. Thank you, Polonca Mali, M.D., Bojan Vindiš, D.M.D., Edita Žugelj, Veronika Saje, Dušan Osojnik, Bhagavata-dharma dasa, Milena Babič, and Igor Pristavec.

I did a lot of research and learning during the creation of this book, and I would like to thank all the experts who inspired me in my work. Among them are: Will Tuttle PhD, Dr. Bruce H. Lipton, Dr. Gabor Maté, Robert H. Lustig, M.D., M.S.L., Joanne Stepaniak, Dr. Sunil V. Joshi, Julian Johnson, Rollin McCraty Ph.D., Paul Roberts, Michael Moss, and Srečko Šorli.

A special thanks goes to everyone who trusted me with their journey of therapeutic fasting and healed their imbalances and illnesses.

# Foreword

## Fasting, the Way to Yourself

I have known Bilka for many years and am interested in which direction her restless spirit leads her on her mission. When I discovered that Bilka had written a new book, I read it with pleasure and passion. In this book, she continues her journey with an in-depth exploration of fasting. Special attention is attracted by scientific findings about fasting, as well as descriptions of similar practices from history.

In the book, both views are skillfully interwoven with many personal experiences and stories from

Bilka's life, giving the additional weight and bringing the topic closer to the reader.

The presentation of the historical development of eating patterns and early forms of fasting and their influence on social events, especially on the spiritual growth of the people of that time, is fascinating. Scientific research is crucial for the modern mind, which needs clear and tangible evidence. That is why the book also describes biochemical processes and changes at the cellular level during fasting, meditation, and other forms of human purification.

Thoughts of this kind are skillfully intertwined so that, despite the progress of science and ever-better knowledge of the functioning of the human body, we return to some fundamental truths. It is knowledge with which the ancient sages already met. Happiness and health are hidden in harmony with the surroundings at a given moment and lead us to this physical and spiritual purity. That is a particular challenge in today's world. There is an ever-widening gap between an overabundance of material goods and a lack of interpersonal relationships and knowledge.

The self-healing potential of the human organism is extraordinary as long as we listen to ourselves carefully. Bilka found her mission precisely in this area, where with proven methods of Ayurveda and fasting tries to direct modern man's attention deep inside and to discover the source of health inside themselves. I, therefore, recommend this book to everyone who is flirting with fasting and would like to learn more about the whole range of beneficial effects it brings.

Bojan Vindiš, Ph.D. dent. Med.

*

Reading the present book by Bilka Baloh is precious. In some places, it starts a gentle climb up the mountain of nutritional knowledge, where one, almost with every step, can discover something instructive and practically applicable. Above all, from the written, the spirit of Bilka's extensive knowledge, her sincerity, frankness, and dedication to the topic under consideration. Her spiritual way is similar to the path we try to follow in the Zen tradition—from the Heart to Heart, not from Mind to Mind.

Dušan Osojnik, Zen Center—Heart of Silence

# Reset

*"There is no logical way to the discovery of these elemental laws. There is only the way of intuition, which is helped by a feeling for the order lying behind the appearance."*
Albert Einstein (1879-1955), German physicist and mathematician[1]

The inner voice, the intuition I faithfully follow because of the current situation, whispered to me that I should write a new book. The book itself called me. I follow the inner impulse, the spontaneous response of my body and spirit. I learned in the past that there are no problems, only how we face them is essential.

That's why I decided to withdraw from the unpleasant atmosphere and melancholy that currently permeate the world. I have thought about this kind of departure for a while, but I didn't know where "my wind" would take me this time. Several times I change the environment, which is vital to me, according to Ayurveda dominant dosha Vata (ether, air). My fantastic constitution at birth, Prakriti in Sanskrit, constantly drives me to dynamism and movement to keep me stable. I will not write about the coronavirus, but about the higher intelligence of which we are all a part. All of us "forge" the future with our thoughts. We shape thoughts into words, words into actions and habits, which eventually become our life. Many people call it fate.

Although I have not had a television for more than 20 years, the information about the coronavirus, which has swept the whole world, follows me every step. Of course, the corona is present and lives in symbiosis with us as it changes and mutates. Fear, sadness, depression, and constant negative information from the media are much bigger enemies than the virus itself. For most of us, a shift in the mind is a true art of letting go of staring, harmful thought patterns and changing them into new and healthy ones. The Eastern doctrine has taught this for thousands of years. We, Westerners, perceive primarily with our minds, and for everything, we need scientific evidence found in neuroscience and epigenetics.

## Departure to Tenerife

My friend and I flew to Tenerife in February 2021 for the general negative vibe. After a few hours, we arrived from the cold and humid Slovenian atmosphere to an entirely new climate and environment. My dominant dosha Vata and winter are not friends because I'm not too keen on humidity and cold winters. I have never been a fan of winter. Maybe as a child, when we still had harsh winters, when there was a lot of snow crunching under the soles of our boots. Even when I was practicing acrobatic skiing, I was cold, but it did not bother me. However, winters are different today, especially wet, humid and gray, a nightmare for me. Last year, on the first of January, I climbed the highest mountain in Slovenia, Triglav, and I am sure this was my last winter ascent to the roof of Slovenia.

I have faced many challenges in my life. Still, socializing has always been the biggest challenge for me, mostly because of complicated interpersonal relationships, the callous attitude of people to animals, resentment, greed, envy between people, and constant conflicts, even in academic spheres.

My parents made me happy the most when I confronted them after thirty years and resolved their disagreements. What a relief! In the past, I have helped many people out of unpleasant situations and re-established broken contacts. The second major challenge was the integrating of the Eastern doctrine of Ayurveda and Western official medicine, which I described in the first book *Fasting, The Seed of Health.* For this book, I have chosen a slightly more complex topic: to connect and present simply the latest scientific research on epigenetics in connection with a meditation on the interdependence between fasting and consciousness and the connection of the mentioned fields.

## Fear and Control

We realize that humans are, at our core, pure consciousness. Pure consciousness is nothing but the field of all possibilities and infinite creativity. Because it is infinite and limitless, it is also complete joy. It could also be called full knowing, endless silence, perfect balance, grace, simplicity, compassion, bliss, or pure love.

When we discover our essence and realize who we are, we already know ourselves because we are nothing but eternal, the possibility, the immeasurable potential of all that was and will be. The law of pure options can also be called the law of unity because all of them are infinite diversity of life-based on the agreement of a single, all-pervading cosmic spirit.

There is no barrier between us and this energy field. We are the field of pure possibility. The more deeply we experience our true nature, the closer we are to the area of pure potential. Experiencing "self" or "self-experiencing" means that the inner point refers to our spirit. This "self-experience" is oriented toward the world and outside us. And not on to the objects from the experiential-material world.

We are constantly subjected to external influences. We are oriented toward the world, into the perceptions and feelings generated by our five senses. We crave approval from others. Our thinking and behavior always act according to the reaction we expect from the environment. The basis of such orientation is, therefore, fear. And fear paralyzes us.

*

If we are oriented toward the external world, we feel a strong need to have things under control. Needs of mastery, approval, and dominance are fear-based needs. Such power is not a valid option for "self-experiencing", which is not pure power. When our experience is not driven by "I am", in us is no fear, no need for control, and longing for approval or external power.The subtle body consists of intellect, mind, and ego. It revolves around the last one. Ego, however, is far from being who we are. Ego is an illusion image imposed on us by a restless and wandering mind. It is the social mask, the role we play. This is a social mask that thrives on the approval of others. Ego wants to control as it is fed by power because it lives in constant fear. Rumi (1207–1273) already wrote: "Instead of fighting the world, kill your ego."[2]

In the Western world, everything must be carefully explained, calculated, and scientifically proven that our mind likes. Finally, science has proved that meditation is a life-changing tool. When we meditate, self-healing the body, mind, and spirit occurs spontaneously. Epigenetics scientifically explains that with the help of a concentration on the breath, we can calm the mind and even change the genetic code.

# Cellular Memory

*"Beliefs are the operating system of the cell, and just like computer software, they can be changed to upgrade the system."*
Dr. Bruce Lipton, American writer and lecturer[3]

## Stress and My Gray Hair

Twenty years ago, I lived in Germany, and life seemed like a box of chocolate. Frankenthal is a beautiful town not far from the university town Heidelberg and Mannheim. I was satisfied. I left in Slovenia, an environment where unforeseen events changed my identity and the spiritual bond with nature I experienced as a child. In Ljubljana, where I lived at the time, I patiently observed people decaying before my eyes.

Moving to Germany seemed like a great solution, but I suddenly found myself in a golden cage on the merry-go-round of abundance. As long as I was a housewife and channeled my love into arranging the "nest", I thought I had found inner peace and what the universe had dedicated to me.

Soon I felt the emptiness and felt like a princess on a golden pea. Nothing more satisfied my needs and desires. I cooked, ironed, cleaned the apartment, walked the dog, traveling around Germany, and went shopping. In short, I did not do anything useful for society and the environment. My creative spirit slowly faded. Soon, even shopping for clothes, shoes, and all kinds of things I did not need at all did not satisfy my dissatisfaction. I wondered about my purpose on this planet, why I was sent, and where I was going. Everything indicated that I was going in the wrong direction.

The partner I lived with was away for days and weeks at a time for a high-level job in a large German multinational. I wondered how to achieve a creative career and live a fulfilling life. I completed a course in Hatha yoga, macrobiotics, and reiki. However, my creative mind was missing something. The child I wanted so much did not come, so I slowly became restless and apathetic. Dissatisfaction soon turned into stress and depression, which I "managed" with various addictions. I started overdoing it with shopping, sports activities and nutrition. The stressful period reached its peak when I realized my partner and I could not have children.

That is when my life turned upside down. Being persistent by nature, I suggested artificial insemination, but a "higher power" had other plans for me. To overcome stress, I practiced yoga daily and flirted with meditation. I was sure that I would get through the crisis period with relaxation and breathing exercises. Unfortunately, I did not find a suitable technique during this period. Guided meditations were not close to me, and no one could present me with a handy tool that would appeal to me.

The weakest link snapped, and the relationship ended dramatically. The stress was taking its toll. In a few months, I got completely gray. A few years later, on the Greek island Leros, I cut off the rest of my gray hair and settled for a gray-haired Bilka.

I accepted the changed image, but my perfectionist mind wanted an answer as to why I had suddenly turned gray. I started researching how the body works in stressful situations and what the consequences are.

## Epigenetics

Epigenetics (epi means outside) is a field of molecular biology that studies changes in an organism's gene expression unrelated to changes in the DNA sequence. It is a chemical modification of the DNA molecule, which can also be inherited in some instances. It represents the realization that environmental factors influence gene expression without changing the DNA record.

As a passionate "mountain freak", I was always stunned that I still reached my goal after a long break and poor condition. Some of the peaks seemed high, but when I got over the first signs of tiredness and continued, I realized that my muscles had an incredible memory. That means every cell has a memory. After the body struggled with fatigue for a while, I understood that the condition of the body and mind are entirely different.

## Can Meditation Change the Genetic Record?

Neuroscientists working in epigenetics have discovered that the chemicals that cause emotions are stored in cell walls. The most prominent representative of epigenetics is the cell biologist Bruce Lipton, who says, among other things, that consciousness can change the genetic record. Advanced relativity is a scientific model that links cosmology, biology, and consciousness and describes how consciousness creates life. Simply put, a conscious person can change their genetic record.

About the benefits of relaxation techniques, Dr. Herbert Benson (1935), an American physician, cardiologist and founder of the Mind-Body Medical Institute at the Massachusetts General Hospital in Boston and a pioneering mind-body researcher, said: "Many studies have shown that mind-body integration such as relaxation and breathing can reduces stress levels, improves health, and prevents adverse clinical effects of stress in conditions such as hypertension, anxiety, diabetes and aging."

## A Mind without a Spirit Is Like a Lamp without Oil

Slovene scientist and researcher Srečko Šorli says biophotonic eating or meditation is a spring of eternal youth. The human body is connected to the soul and spirit through the bioenergetic body, consisting of biophotons. The leading scientist in this field is the German physicist Dr. Fritz Alfred Popp, who says that every living organism accumulates and emits biophotons. Biophotons are an information system between individual cells of an organism and a medium for transmitting information between the organism and its surroundings. Šorli describes consciousness as an infinite dimensional space in areas with fewer dimensions. The physical space in which the material universe and life are three-dimensional. The cosmic mind is four- and multi-dimensional.

"Matter and mind exist in consciousness. Consciousness creates life in a three-dimensional reality by using the pilot biophotons of the higher regions of the mind. Pilot biophotons guide photons in three-dimensional reality so that energy is created at the molecular level. When a person achieves consciousness and becomes one with it, he can consciously change his genetic record with the help of pilots of biophotons."

A person who meditates regularly and is deep in consciousness can change the genetic record through pilot biophotons. When the 3D-biophoton connects with the 9D-pilot biophoton, the 9D-space, which in yoga corresponds to the Ajna chakra—the third eye, can transfer 84 bits of information into the micro tube. That is, it moves the corresponding data to the 28 triads in the micro tube, which then polypeptides move up to 28 DNA triads.

With this, consciousness "resets" the genetic record and creates a new one. It is also possible for a mind unrelated to consciousness to create a false DNA record. Most of today's diseases are psychosomatic, as they originate in the improper functioning of the mind. A mind that is not connected to consciousness cannot function properly. A mind without consciousness is like a charioteer without reins.[4]

*

Eastern philosophy has been teaching this for thousands of years. The interpretation of the inner worlds can also be called dimensions. We cannot perceive or see it with our eyes. We are talking about the astral, causal, and super causal world. These are the areas or dimensions from where we came from. We are made out of energy, light, sound, and word (Naam in the Sanskrit language). We can see the inner worlds when we reach consciousness through meditation. Some people call this state enlightenment.

Sources state that the average adult human body consists of 50 trillion cells, while others lean toward 10 trillion. The scientific website, Science NetLinks, a tool for science teachers, notes that the cells in the human body are approximately 100 trillion. In any case, there are too many to count. The matter is even more difficult because of cellular processes, and the number of cells constantly changes. Some fail, and others are restored. So also, the number of cells is not constant in the body, and we will probably never know how many cells it makes us up.

A human being develops from a single fertilized egg cell, which has in heredity records all information for the structure and functioning of the organism. All cell organisms have the same inheritance at the starting point, which the father and mother—in contributed Ayurveda we call it Prakriti.

In successive cell divisions, the number of cells increases strongly and rapidly. New cells can only be formed by dividing the existing ones. After division, the two cells may be identical or different according to the structure and the role they perform. Cells from which cells of other tissues can develop are called stem cells. The outer part of the cell is the cell membrane, in which there are channels through which substances are exchanged with the environment. The contents of the cell—the cytoplasm—are an aqueous mixture, a solution of various substances (water, salt, proteins, fats, sugars, and others), and it contains cell inclusions (organelles). Every cell must maintain itself, but at the same time, it participates in the maintenance of the whole organism.

The fact is that every cell has a memory.

# Mechanisms for the Survival

*"All truth passes through three stages. First, it is ridiculed. Second, it is violently opposed. Third, it is accepted as being self-evident."*
Arthur Schopenhauer (1788-1860), German philosopher[5]

Evolution gifted us several mechanisms for survival, among which growth and protection are most exposed and essential. We can all probably agree that protection and defense are vital, but for our life is necessary as well as growth. In our body, billions of cells are worn out daily, which the body has to replace. They have to grow anew. In the microbiome, for example, cells are replaced every 72 hours.

"When Dr. Bruce H. Lipton cloned human endothelial cells, he gave them into the culture vessel, and the cells moved away from the toxins. Similar to how people withdraw from unpleasant events.

These cells move toward nutrients, just as we go for lunch or to pleasant events. Those opposing movements determine two primary cellular responses to environmental stimuli. Scrolling to save the signal of life, for example, nutrients, is characteristic of the growth response; scrolling away from threatening signals, such as toxins, is typical of a defensive response.

These opposite survival mechanisms, which have evolved billions of years, cannot work simultaneously. The cells cannot be scrolling forward and backward at the same time. Dr. Lipton proved that the cells in human blood vessels showed one microscopic anatomy behind providing nutrients and another to give a defensive response. However, they could not handle both configurations at the same time. So we have two opposing, shifting cellular responses.

The growth processes require an exchange between the organism and the environment. When, for example, we eat food and then excrete waste matter—feces. On the other hand, the defense mechanism stops the system from protecting the organism from the environmental threat it perceives.

Inhibition of growth processes exhausts the body also because growth is a process that not only consumes energy but also has to produce it. At the same time, the body's constant defense response inhibits the generation of life-sustaining energy. The longer we stay in a defensive state, the more we jeopardize our growth.

The proportion of cells in the defense response depends on the threat's severity. When we are under stress, we can survive, but chronic inhibition of growth mechanisms seriously threatens our vitality. To stay healthy is not enough to get rid of stress. To develop correctly, we must actively strive for joyful, loving, and fulfilling lives that encourage growth.

Growth and defense processes in multicellular organisms are controlled by the nervous system. This, however, depends on the signals from the environment, which are interpreted and organized into appropriate behavioral responses. This is reflected and based on the five senses. When the nervous system recognizes threatening stress from the environment, the community of cells is alerted to impending danger.[6]"

## Chronic Stress and Inflammation Processes

The fast rhythm of life forces us constantly on standby state. In that case, the body is always in a fight-flight state. This condition is called chronic stress, which reduces the function of the immune system. Disruption of immune receptors causes an imbalance called glucocorticoid receptor resistance (GRO), in which the intensity of inflammation increase with the duration and intensity of stress. That increases the risk of asthma and other autoimmune diseases while promoting the onset and progression of chronic inflammatory diseases such as rheumatoid arthritis, heart disease, and cancer. GRO is also associated with people who experience chronic stress at work, parents of children with cancer, spouses of cancer patients, and people who suffer from extreme loneliness.

With this explanation, I finally got an answer why I went utterly gray in a short time. For many years I lived in a constant state of fight or flight. Repetitive stress turned me from a redhead into a gray-haired one. There are no shortcuts on the path of transformation.

Today, I am delighted with my gray hair. Besides, I don't have to dye my hair every month and save valuable time. That is how Mother Nature wants me, and it will stay that way.

*

Despite unpleasant side effects, drugs are still a biomedical solution for stress and anxiety. In recent times, scientists have reported superior results on the effectiveness of drug-free healing, leading to the revival of energy healing techniques known for thousands of years. Numerous studies by independent experts and scientists have confirmed that the "relaxation" response, which researchers define as a physiological and psychological state, alleviates symptoms of anxiety and other psychological disorders. Relaxation affects heart rate, blood pressure, oxygen consumption, and brain activity. A groundbreaking study published in 2013, shows, that the physiological state of deep relaxation can achieve through meditation, yoga, breathing exercises (pranayama), and prayer, that is, by concentrating on one's inner experiences.

## The Defense Mechanisms

"The body has several defense mechanisms, but two are the most important. The first system mobilizes the defense against external threats. It is the axis between the hypothalamus, pituitary gland, and adrenal gland. This axis is inactive when we are not in danger, and growth is excellent.

When the hypothalamus in the brain detects danger in the environment, the axis is activated. It signals the pituitary gland, the primary gland responsible for managing 50 billion cells, for dealing with impending danger. Hypothalamus recognizes signals from the environment, and the pituitary gland stimulates the functioning of the body's organs. In response to environmental threats, the pituitary gland alerts the adrenal glands to initiate a fight-flight state.

Stress hormones give us tremendous physical strength to run away from danger. When the brain registers a threat, the hypothalamus releases corticotrophin, which travels to the pituitary gland. Corticotrophin activates special hormone-secreting cells, causing them to release adrenocorticotropic hormones into the blood. These travel to the adrenal glands, which signal to start the secretion of adrenal hormones for fight-flight.

When stress hormones are released into the blood, the blood vessels of the digestive tract constrict the tract and force the energy-providing blood to feed hand and foot tissues preferentially. Limbs allow us to move away from danger. The blood was before accumulated in the internal organs. The arrangement of blood from the viscera ultimately halts growth-related functions. Without nutrients from the blood, the internal organs cannot function optimally. The body stops performing its tasks of maintaining life, digestion, absorption of nutrients, secretions, and others, that ensure cell growth and produce energy reserves in the body. Thus, stress inhibits growth processes and endangers the body's survival by stopping the production of vital energy reserves in the organs and tissues."

*

"Another defense system of the body is the immune system. It protects us from threats caused by bacteria and viruses. When the immune system is heavily burdened, it uses up most of the body's energy reserves. We feel this when we get minor infections such as angina, flu, or common colds. The stress mentioned above, hormones have a devastating effect on the immune system. The brain has to decide what a more significant threat is, microbes in the microbiome or danger from the outside. The body prioritizes the flow of energy for fight and survival response coming from the environment rather than for destroying microbes that can infect our body."

## The Most Important Is Biochemistry

"Our capacity to feel reward and satisfaction is a mechanical reading of neurochemical processes in us—Neuroscientist Dr. Robert Lustig studied neurons grown in Petri dishes. During his years of work, he gained a unique insight into the relationship between hormones and behavior. He took neurons and hormones (estradiol, testosterone, cortisol) and observed how the neurons 'go crazy'.

These processes are the basis of aggression, passivity, maternal instinct, sexual orientation, and identity. Our behavior is the result of individual neural connections. In every individual, it comes from the same basic principle—biochemistry.

Lustig says he doesn't see people's behavior and emotions but neural pathways and biochemistry. For example, he cites the decline in school success, which he understood as inefficient brain mitochondria. When we notice the sudden worsening of diabetes, he sees fat accumulation in the liver and muscles, leading to insulin resistance. Where we see drug abuse, he sees presynaptic transporters and postsynaptic receptors. When we see teenagers 'glued' to their smartphones, Lustig sees prefrontal cortex dysfunction, the brain area that regulates the maintenance of attention. Where we see the effect, Lustig considers the cause.[7]"

*

Hundreds of areas in the brain have evolved to perform different functions. The frontal lobe controls muscle movement. The occipital lobe allows vision. The occipital lobe enables hearing. The limbic or emotional part of the brain manages the center of our emotions—laughter, crying, and fear.

The brain consists of billions of neurons—nerve cells that constantly communicate with each other through a complex neural network. Each neuron has a cell body that produces proteins to keep it alive and neurotransmitters, the nerve messengers that allow neurons to communicate with each other. Each neuron also has an axon, a nerve fiber that transmits information. Each neuron has dendrites, special outgrowths with which it receives data, and on each of them, there are many receptors. Neurotransmitters and receptors are like keys that fit with specific locks.

*

The limbic system of the brain, or the system that "regulates" emotions, consists of three main systems. These send and receive chemical information that translates into positive or negative emotions. These are the reward, satisfaction, stress, fear, and memory systems.

"The first system—the reward system—consists of neurons synthesizing the neurotransmitter dopamine. When the neurons are triggered, they send dopamine to another brain area. That is the area of feelings, emotions, and motivation. The neurons then release a set of neurochemicals called endogenous opioid peptides, which have the same effect on the brain as morphine or heroin and produce pleasure, a feeling of bliss or euphoria. The dopamine neurons' nucleus quickly detects pleasure, such as uncontrolled shopping, alcohol, overeating, masturbation, smoking, and drugs.

The second system is the satisfaction system. That uses a neurotransmitter call it serotonin to communicate between neurons in the dorsal nucleus and other places in the cerebral cortex, where the brain interprets impulses as 'good' or 'bad'. Researchers have recently found that more than 70% of serotonin is produced in the gut microbiome.

The third brain system is the stress, fear, and memory system. Four brain areas are involved in it. Amygdala is the center of stress and fear. The hypothalamus at the base of the brain regulates all of our body's hormones, including the stress hormone cortisol, which prepares our body for extreme stress. If necessary, it also communicates with the sympathetic nervous system (fight-flight response) and the vagus nerve. Hippocampus is the brain's center for memory and learning. It stores memories, both pleasant and unpleasant. The fourth area is the prefrontal cortex. That is the wisdom area of the brain. It prevents us from repeating stupid things that could endanger us. These four areas of the brain ensure that our emotions do not paralyze our ability to think clearly and behave. We can say that they regulate our attitude toward our surroundings.[8]"

These three central systems govern all our emotions, especially those related to reward and pleasure.

# The Wandering of the
# Scattered Mind

*"Conquer your mind and Conquer the world."*
Guru Nanak (1469–1539), the founder of Sikhism[9]

While traveling in Italy for a few years, I borrowed Julian Johnson's book, Path of the Masters, from a friend who lives in Trieste. I read it quickly and immediately decided on a spiritual path called Surat Shabd yoga—the yoga of the audible life stream.

At first, it seemed that the path skillfully dodged to me. That happened a few years later when I met a group in Ljubljana that practiced this kind of meditation. I haven't found people in Italy who deal with this meditation technique. But I didn't worry too much because I left most things to my intuition. It'll be there when I'm ready.

## Meditation—Concentration

"When we venture into the inner worlds and focus on all that resides within us, we bring the mind down to the coherence of the heart, to the fluttering of the heart. Coherence of the heart refers to the interconnectedness of the spirit with the brain. Neuroradiology has discovered that the heart has its internal nervous system—a network of nerves so functionally sophisticated that we can speak of the brain of the heart'. This cerebellum contains more than 41,000 neurons, enabling the heart to independently perceive, process information, make decisions, and influence learning and memory.[10]

Physician and scientist Rollin McCarty, director of HeartMath Institute Research, says the heart is an intelligent system. Research has revealed that the heart is a hormone gland that produces and secretes many hormones and neurotransmitters that strongly influence brain function and body. Among the hormones produced by the heart is also oxytocin—known as a 'love hormone' or 'bonding hormone'. Science is just beginning to understand the effects of electromagnetic fields produced by the heart. There is evidence that the information of a strong heart plays an essential synchronizing role in the human body and affects the people we come into contact with."

*

"Electrophysiological studies conducted at the HeartMath Institute have proven that the heart plays a crucial role in intuition. They have shown that the heart is a key component of the emotional system. Scientists now understand that the heart not only responds to emotions but that the signals generated by its rhythmic activity play an essential role in determining the quality of the moment-to-moment emotional experience. These cardiac signals also strongly affect perception and cognitive functioning due to the extensive communication network between the heart and the brain.[11]"

## Concentration

"There are different meditation techniques. Concentrating on the breath and keywords (mantras) can bring the mind to the center. We must completely forget about the outside world. As long as the mind "wanders" in the external world, we cannot climb higher. We must close all nine doors to the outside world to succeed—eyes, ears, nostrils, mouth, genitals, and anus. Through these openings, we communicate with the outside world. We focus our thoughts on the inner center by excluding the outer world. Contact with the inner world starts in the area of the third eye. There begins a higher concentration. When we gather all the rays of attention in this place, and when no thoughts arise in us anymore, we begin to taste the results of meditation. These are inevitable."

*

"First, we see flashes of light and hear all sorts of sounds. No matter what we see or hear, we must remain focused on the center and the breath—in other words, we should never listen to sound or light from the outside world. Sound and light must come to the center from within. If we leave the center, we will lose sound and light. Collecting concentration in the center, the power of the mind is extinguished, but the power of the soul is increasing.

When the concentration grows to the maximum possible level, the soul has enough power to open the tenth gate. This gate is located in the finer body, near the center of the head. First, we can only look through this door. We can gradually overcome them with training and repetition and leave the body entirely. This world is a kind of astral realm, part of a universe that lies just above the physical world, which means a new dimension for us. We can call it the fourth dimension, but it is not precisely defined. It is different for each individual. Every one of us has a different experience."

*

"In this immense universe, there are an infinite number of dimensional worlds, one higher than the other. Each world or group of worlds is divided into higher and lower. The level of vibration separates these. People cannot see certain worlds as the areas there are much above and below the level that our field of vision can reach since the eyes are adapted to the environment in which we live. Because of this, we cannot see the astral worlds with our physical eyes. But with our eyes, we can see them as distinctly as the material world surrounding us. It is the same with the higher worlds. Each higher world or group of dimensions has a more significant and different light, color, beauty, and happiness, which is tasted by all who reach this realm.[12]"

It takes a lot of experience and practice for the door into the pure consciousness open to us. An experienced teacher can help us. Take us from one level to another, to the final dimension. We cannot go this way alone. Only an experienced person can help us with consecration and initiation. Practicing without blessing does not bear fruit.

"We cannot get this knowledge from books. On the contrary, we can be exposed to unpredictable dangers. We get out of the karmic net only with the help of a living teacher."

Jesus taught: "Do not look for laws in the holy scriptures, because life itself is a law. The paper itself is dead. The law is a living word given to the people by a living prophet." This law is written in everything that lives. You will find it in the grass, the tree and the river, the birds in the sky, and the fish in the lake and the sea—but search for it, above all within yourself. The Creator did not write laws in the pages of your books but in your hearts and spirit. They are written in your breath, your blood, your flesh, your guts, your eyes and ears, and in every smallest part of your body. They are constantly present in the air, water, earth, plants, sunlight, and in depths and heights. They do you no good to diligently read dead scriptures while your works deny the one who gave them to you. There is no gluttony in the records you carry, nor is there any licentiousness and lust, nor is their lust for wealth or hatred of your enemies. All this comes from the kingdom of darkness, the demon prince, the prince of evil Beelzebub."

*

Suppose we are persistent and practice meditation daily. In that case, the system will help the spiritual exercises take us over the "threshold of death" into the realm beyond death, from where we came voluntarily. Samadhi, the highest level of concentration beyond any awareness, takes the individual through and beyond the end. However, without "dharma", taming of the passions, and the subjugation of the mind, it is impossible. The original meaning of dharma is 'natural law'. The root word, Dham, means 'to support'. We can say that dharma is what supports the natural order of the universe. The truth, we call it love and compassion.

Some of the world's great thinkers who knew this kind of experience were familiar with this secret. Plutarch wrote: "The soul at death experiences similar impressions and has passed through a similar process to those who are initiated into the great mystery."

And how does meditation affect fasting? The answer is in the flow body. It is easiest to stop the mind when the body is clean, purified, flowing, and light. During fasting, we only consume mild herbal teas, warm water, clear water soups, and perform Basti (enema), allowing the body to bring the mind to the center more quickly. Overabundance is the saturation of the body with the juices of solid food that burdens the body and mind. Meditation was weak then, and the so-called self-healing could not occur, not even enlightenment.

# The Essenes—First Philosophers on Fasting

*"As long as Man continues to be the ruthless destroyer of lower living beings, he will never know health or peace. For as long as men massacre animals, they will kill each other. Indeed, he who sows the seed of murder and pain cannot reap joy and love."*
Pythagoras (6th century BC), Greek philosopher and mathematician[13]

"Arnold Toynbee (1889-1975), a world-renowned cultural theorist and philosopher of history, who headed the Royal Institute of International Affairs in

London wrote, "that the Essenes were the most authentic group of philosophers in human history. However, they appeared long before that. The first records were found around 150 BC in the eastern Mediterranean. Two thousand years ago, around 4000 of them lived to very old age, up to 120 years. At that time, the average age in Palestine was 30 to 35 years.

The Essenes were recognized for wearing white linen clothes, distinguished from ordinary woolen ones. So their clothes were not of animal origin either. The New Testament of the Bible mentions them as people in white dresses or people 'on the way'. They also called them Ebionites, poor, or the Nazoreans, who regularly practiced fasting and meditation and had a special vow to abstain from 'bloody' food. They rejected temple sacrifices and eating meat. They were doctors and prophets. The main center of the Essenes was on Mount Carmel in northwestern Israel. The Egyptian Essenes, whose center was near Lake Mareotis, are also known. These were doctors and therapists. The word is derived from Theravada and means young Buddhist monks sent to Egypt by the Indian king Ashoka (268-232 BC). Their job was to heal the people and animals.

The Essenes were studied by the Jewish historian Philo (25 BC-40 AD). He wrote that the Essenes ate once a day, namely in the evening. Eating food was a ritual for them, to which they dedicated much attention. They gratefully accepted Mother Earth's gifts and thanked the meals. The food was bloodless, and dinner was called the Holy Supper.

We can say that the Essenes were the first Pythagoreans or Buddhists. The Greek philosopher Pythagoras from the 6th century BC created a plan for how humanity should live healthily and progress, with a changed way of eating. He was inspired by Buddha, whom he is said to have met in India. Pythagoras' epistle was unequivocal and, among other things, expressed his love for animals. That means that it is not allowed to kill and eat them. This commandment comes from the doctrine of reincarnation, the law of karma, and the law of cause and effect. Pythagoras also relied on Orpheus, the mythological Greek singer who charmed animals and trees with his music. Orpheus calmed the frightened animal world with his music and carried a lamb on his shoulders, which means he wanted to help animals with love."

*

"Two thousand years after Pythagoras, the great Leonardo da Vinci (1452-1519), another genius whose art and inventions helped the beginning of the Renaissance, spoke that people should not eat animals. Our society ignored his far-sighted words about the severe consequences of our diet: "I gave up meat at a young age, and the time will come when people will look at killing animals the way they look at killing people.

Leonardo was a sworn vegetarian—a Pythagorean. He painted oranges on the plates at the Last Supper, even though oranges were unknown in Italy two thousand years ago. Leonardo knew this because, in his time, they were brought from distant lands and began cultivating in Europe. He wanted to point out that Jesus recommended the best Mother Earth has to offer the human race for the Holy Supper."

## The Discovery of the Essenes Gospel of Peace

"Prof. Dr. Edmond Bordeaux Szekely discovered the Essene Epistle of Peace. He translated and interpreted the Qumran manuscripts found at the Dead Sea in 1947, the Zend Avesta, and the Pre-Columbian Writings of Ancient Mexico. Szekely received his doctorate from the University of Paris and other academic titles in Vienna and Leipzig. He taught philosophy and cultural psychology at the University of Cluj and was recognized for his research into ancient languages—Sanskrit, Armenian, Greek, and Latin. He was a polyglot, as he spoke ten languages of this period.

He found an Old Slavonic text in the royal library of the Habsburgs in Vienna and transcribed it. In

Rome, he found out that the text is a literal translation of the Essene manuscripts from Armenian. As a doctor, he considered that the statements about human health were significant that man most urgently needs. In 1937, he published the first copy of the text in London, which was translated into 50 languages.[14]" Essenes monks were ancient philosophers who lived in the caves of Qumran where the Dead Sea Scrolls were discovered.

*

The Swiss philosopher and Gandhi's friend Werner Zimmermann published a German translation of this epistle in 1939. Before him, the Nobel laureate Romain Rolland (1915-1944) stare to spread the Essene way of life and strove to bring the nations together. It felt in his voluminous biographies of Beethoven, Michelangelo, Tolstoy, and Gandhi, who were vegetarians according to his belief.

*

"Leo Nikolayevich Tolstoy (1828-1910) wrote the book Pervaja Stupenj (The First Step) in 1892, which has similar content to the Essene Epistle of Peace. However, he could not have known it, as Szekley only discovered it in 1923 in the Vatican. "In 1901, Tolstoy was excommunicated from the Orthodox Church because of his natural conception of the Eucharist—the Holy Supper, which should be healthy and bloodless.[15]"

Slovenian greatest poet, France Prešeren (1800-1849), found that in his time, Slovenians did not have any natural classical Essene-Pythagorean philosophers. With the aphorism he wrote, he hit the heart of unpleasant times: "Golden times would have already come to the Slovenes if not every writer talks nonsense to us was considered a classic.[16]"

*

"The Pythagoreans believed that if we eat the meat of killed animals, the demon soul enters us. That is why they forbade eating meat. Others saw demons at work only in certain animals. They believed, for example, that a demon that causes epilepsy hides in goat meat. The pork was forbidden because it was said to cause skin diseases and increase sexual desire. Fasting was supposed to purify oneself. In the past, it was fasting protected people from demons and disease.

Most of the information about the Essenes goes to the Jewish historian Josephus Flavius (Josephus Flavius, 37-100 AD), who came from the priestly nobility and lived with the Essenes for three years.

In the Book of Adam, Ethiopian manuscripts, we can read that the animal is not killed by the righteous Abel but by Cain. The Bible says exactly the opposite, so the consciousness of the ban on killing animals is lost. The third son of Adam, Seth, begged his father to show him a righteous life with bloodless sacrifices. The descendants of Cain, the Cainites, were murderous. They introduced noise music, hunting, and wars. Set's descendants, the Setites, kept the commandment of eating fruit with medicinal seeds. This commandment was given to humanity by the creator—Elohim.[17]"

## Cleansing with Fasting

"The philosopher and "anti-pope" Hippolytus (died 235) reported how according to the Setite tradition, Jesus washed and fasted himself with clean running water and drank it as much as he could. Today we know that with fasting, a new divine life begins, which is reflected in the flexibility of the cells, better well-being, more beautiful skin, and significant shifts also occur on the spiritual level. Fasting eliminates the slavery of old habits, dependence, and addiction.[18]"

*

Following the example of the Essenes and their most prominent representative, Jesus, we should have to heal with the help of air, sun, water, and food, which was prepared for us by a higher intelligence. We can call them angels, gods, God, or Mother Earth with her helpers. It is time to raise awareness that our creators and followers gave us the Earth and healthy fruits. The Essene Epistle of Peace emphasizes that they were given to us for health and happiness, fruits that have seeds inside.

It is known that kernels of apricots, bitter almonds, peaches, and plums prevent the formation of cancerous formations that threaten all civilized humankind. These kernels contain vitamin B17, which is called laetrile or amygdalin. With seeds containing vitamin B17 in the past, they also treated deadly diseases such as scurvy, beriberi disease, and pernicious anemia. The Chinese treated cancer in this way already 1500 years ago. The first in writing a report on this comes from the year 502.

*

In the 1950s, Dr. Ernst Krebs (1911-1996) found that laetrile prevents cancer. The news has been spreading in recent years despite opposition from the pharmaceutical industry and the political organizations that live off this insidious disease.

Papaya, mango, and pineapple contain excellent enzymes. Soon after, when Dr. Renato Buzzonetti

(1924-2017), a personal physician of Pope Wojtyla, passed away, and Wojtyla began to suffer from Parkinson's disease. In June 2002, Dr. Pramentier recommended daily consumption of papayas, and the late Pope made a significant recovery[19].

*

In Mother Earth's pharmacy, we have well-known effective medicines, but now we are rediscovering them again. Among them are bitter cucumber, Momordica charantia, which can be used to treat diabetes successfully, and Canadian Essence tea, a collection of eight medicinal herbs used by Canadian Indians to treat cancer. Also important are the watermelon's seeds and juice, which dissolve bile and other stones.

*

The stevia sweetener is as much as 200 times stronger than ordinary sugar. Stevia is excellent for weight loss, improves skin and hair, heart, liver, and stomach, helps in addictions, and in combination with manganese, it strengthens the bones and cartilage of the spine, which at first glance is quite incredible. At the same time, it is also a medicine: it regulates blood pressure, hypoglycemia, candida, depression, and colds, protects teeth and gums, and improves hair. Stevia in South Amerika It has been used in countless recipes. Also been used in Japan for centuries and has no side effects.

*

It's impressive and delicious Jerusalem artichoke, which is much sweeter than potatoes and undemanding to grow.

Returning to nature and natural eating will undoubtedly be difficult and slow. Starting with personal cleansing and organic food on healthy hummus will be necessary. We are faced with going back to nature or our negligent handling of the environment, especially animals, which will force Earth to shake off its parasites forcefully, primarily humans. Mainly because of the consumers who consume contaminated bloody food and live almost all over the world. We are free to decide to cleanse ourselves internally, or we will be cleansed from the 'outside'. Voluntarily the inner cleansing is beautiful and joyful, but the outer will be very bitter (hunger, diseases, wars, premature death)[20].

In southern England, aliens are in the wheat fields. In addition to symbolic messages wrote: "We are not alone." We are not the only ones who read this message on Earth, and those who wrote it down for us, are not alone.

**Cleanse yourself by fasting, and the angel of air, water and the sun will help you**

## From the Essene Gospel of Peace:

1. Renew and fast because I tell you the truth; you can get rid of Satan and his evil deeds only by fasting, prayer, and meditation.
2. Go and fast privately; do not allow anyone to see you fasting. The living God will see you, and the reward will be great.
3. Fast as long as Beelzebub—the prince of evil spirits, with all his evil spirits, does not leave your body until all the angels come, our Mother Earth, and serve you.
4. If you do not fast, you will never be free from Satan's power and diseases that come from him.
5. While you fast, avoid the sons of men. Seek company angels of Mother Earth. Whoever seeks will find.
6. Look for the fresh air of forests and fields, for in such a place, you will find the angel of AIR.
7. Undress and allow the angel of air to embrace your body.
8. Then breathe slowly and deeply so that the angel of air can permeate you from the inside.

9.    Angel of air will drive out all the impurities the mind has polluted from outside and inside.

10.   Thus, all that is foul and unclean will depart from you, like the smoke of a fire that goes up and is lost in the sea of air.

11.   Then find the angel of WATER.

12.   Take off your shoes, lay down your clothes, and allow the angel of water to hug your body.

13.   I tell you the truth, the angel of the water will wash everything out of your body, the impurities that soiled you from outside and inside. All impure or the stench will flow far away from you, as it washes away the dirt from the clothes when washed in the river and lost in its flow.

14.   All must be renewed with water and truth, for your bodies are they bathe in the river of earthly life, and your spirit flows in the river of eternal life. You have received blood from Mother Earth and truth from the One Heavenly Father.

15.   Your inner dirt is even more than your outer dirt. He who cleanses himself only from the outside but inside remains dirty. It is like a grave, which is beautifully plastered on the outside, but the inside is full of hideous filth and abominations.

16.   Allow the angel of water to baptize you from the inside, to free you from all past sins so that the inside of your body will also be as clean as the spray foam of a stream playing in the sun.

17. So look for a larger pumpkin with a stem as long as your husband's height. Dispose of its contents and fill it with the river water you used earlier warmed in the sun. Hang it on a tree branch, get down on your knees in front of the angel of water, and insert the stem into your buttock so the water will easily pour into your bowels.

18. Kneel on the ground and pray to the living God to forgive you all past sins, and ask the angel of water to free you from all dirt and all diseases.

19. Then release the water from your body to wash away all the dirt and Satan's stench. And you will see with your own eyes and smell with your nose abominations and filth that have defiled the sanctuary of your body and right so the sins that dwelt in your body and you in all possible ways suffered with pain.

20. Internal water baptism will save you from all these evils.

21. Repeat this baptism every day of your fast until you see that the water flowing from you is as pure as the foam of a gurgling stream. Then go in the flowing river; in the embrace of an angel, give thanks to the living God who saved you from your sins.

22. This holy baptism with the angel of water signifies rebirth into new life.

23. For then, your eyes will see, and your ears will hear.

24. After this baptism, sin no more, that the angels of air and water may be light eternally residing in you and serving you.

25. But if traces of your past sins and impurities remain in you, look for the angel of SUNLIGHT.

26. Take off your shoes, put away your clothes, and allow the angel of the sun to embrace your body.

27. Breathe with long and deep breaths to be an angel of sunlight that could penetrate you. He will cast out from you all that is foul and unclean that is in you defiled from without and from within.

28. Everything stinking and dirty will be chased away from you as the rising sun's brightness chases away the night's darkness.

29. Everyone must be reborn with sunlight and truth, for the body warmed by the sunshine of your Mother Earth and your spirit, the sunshine of the truth of the Heavenly Creator.

30. The angels of air, water, and sunlight are your brothers.

31. May all three angelic brothers hug and stay with you throughout the cleansing.

32. For verily I say unto you, the power of evildoers, all sins and impurity will immediately leave your body if embraced by these three angels.

33. When the angels of Mother Earth conquer your
bodies to such an extent that the lords of the
temple may again rule it. Evil will be loathed by
all scents the body will leave, either by breathing
or through the skin, with water through your
mouth or skin, your buttocks, and genitals.

34. And all this you will see with your eyes and
smell with your nose and fingers.

35. When all sins and impurities have gone far from
you, your blood will stand as pure as the blood
of Mother Earth, like the playful foam of a river
in sunlight.

36. And your breath will become as pure as the
breath of tar flowers[21].

37. Your breath, your blood, your flesh will again be
one with your Mother Earth, and then your spirit
will also be able to become one again with the
spirit of the Heavenly Father[22].

# Abundance against Hunger



*"Sooner or later, everyone sits down to a banquet of consequences."*
Robert Louis Stevenson (1850-1894), Scottish writer and poet[23]

A broader view of human history is needed to understand the overabundance of food on one side and the hunger of more than a billion people on the other side. Moreover, the population increased in the last millennia. Over a while ago, our civilization was threatened with extinction due to a lack of food for centuries. People were increasingly malnourished and sick, and food they did not produce enough. Today, the situation does not look much better with all the technology and mechanization.

## The Neglected Role of the Environment

If Darwin's evolutionary theory, his successors, historians, and anthropologists who studied human development are to be believed, the population began to grow with the first 'agricultural revolution'.

However, Charles Darwin admitted he neglected the role of the environment in the theory of evolution. In 1876, he wrote a letter to Moritz Wagner: "In my opinion, the biggest mistake is that I have done it in my life, was not to allow sufficient weight to the direct effect of the environment, food, climate and so on, independent of natural selection. When I wrote On the Origin of Species, and for several years afterward, I found little good evidence of direct environmental influence. Still, there is considerable evidence" (C. Darwin, 1888).

*

"The agricultural revolution began in different parts of the world from 12,000 to 8,000 years. There was a thaw, and our ancestors began to move toward the north because of the need to survive. Due to favorable weather conditions, crops grew better and better, and there was more and more food. Smaller and faster gazelles and antelopes entered the savanna area and roe deer, which our ancestors only hunted with difficulty. They invented the arrow for shooting at smaller and quicker targets, but they could not retain the previous hunting lifestyle with these tools. They began supplementing their diet by gathering nuts, strawberries, peas, barley, and wheat.

During this time, small groups of people cultivated wheat, barley (Central Asia), rice (Middle East), maize (Central America), and tuber. Around 8000 BC, humans domesticated goats, sheep, pigs, and cattle, even though these lean animals were raised solely for milk and hides and not because of the meat. We can say that farming was more manageable and redeeming for our ancestors. The people of that time knew about plants and their power[24] from the time of gathering. They knew wheat and barley were edible, and the seeds sprouted again. In addition, from their hunting past, they had an incredible social arrangement, which is undoubtedly necessary for such a great project as farming."


## Kurgans and Fenced Livestock

Ten thousand years ago, nomadic tribes from the Kurdish mountains began c to domesticate wild animals in northeastern Iraq. As archaeologist Marija Gimbutas (1921-1994) calls them, Kurgan peoples started to invade Eastern Europe from Central Asia and the Mediterranean area seven thousand years ago. They brought with them a bloodthirsty attitude toward animals. Anthropologists hypothesize that hunting became widespread when our ancestors began to fence certain herds of wild sheep and feed on them. Soon after, they domesticated goats, and two thousand years later cows, horses, and camels.

## The Growth of the Population

Over time, our ancestors learned to grind grain, cook it into porridge, and prepare bread. That increases the nutritional and caloric value of meals. They started to feed children with porridge, and mothers stopped breastfeeding faster because of the increasingly high-calorie food. From before four years, breastfeeding was halved to two, which also halved the period between births. The population began to grow. From about five million people who, according to anthropologists' estimates, should live in the world twelve thousand years ago, the number increased to seven thousand years ago twenty million.

## Food—A Source of Military and Political Power

Around 3500 BC, farming became a source of power. Wealth accumulated in Mesopotamia and Egypt, and this was the beginning of the first shop for money. The first money and form of capital were sheep, goats, and cows, as they were the only edible property of tangible value. Also, The English word "capital" comes from the word capita, which in Latin means "head" and was used in the past for counting livestock.

Food surpluses allowed people to engage with other crafts: they baked bread and pastries, built buildings, brewed beer, blacksmithing, and many others. Social inequality appeared for the first time, the very one that undermines the healthy roots of humanity and its existence even today.

The population overgrew. Food was becoming part of the military and political power. The most obvious example is the fall of the Roman Empire in the fourth century. The Romans obtained wheat from distant Asia and Africa, but their food system also collapsed with the collapse of military power. The Western food economy sank so profoundly that in the next six centuries, the world's population from three hundred million increased only to three hundred and ten million.

*

The agricultural system began to recover again around the year one thousand with the help of extraordinary inventions that increased yields. They started with crop rotation. They invented a new, deeper plow, and the soil was enriched with animal manure. They learned to choose the most vital seeds for further sowing plants and thus gradually improved the quality of the plants. With these technological approaches, trade also accelerated.

The farmer grew what he could best earn. Enterprising traders planted large plantations of sugar cane and tea in tropical countries. Food began to change from a necessity to a commodity. They produced as much as they needed for survival, but it was becoming a passionate race for profit. Farmers and merchants tried to increase production and reduce covered costs.

Between 1300 and 1600, the grain yield almost doubled. Therefore meat production and consumption increased. In the sixteenth century, the average German ate a quarter of a kilo of meat daily; in Europe, even farm workers ate meat at least once a day. That meant more and more calories, and the result was population growth.

*

Between 1500 and 1750, the population increased from 500 to 800 million. Agriculture at this time was burdened by ever-increasing numbers of people and the mass production of livestock. The need for grain, hay, and other feed rapidly increased. A cow has to eat seven kilograms of feed to gain one kilogram of body weight. Similar was with to pigs and chickens. Until there were only a few people per hectare living on European land, there were no problems, but when the land was plowed into fields due to lack of food, the food system collapsed[25].

*

"In 1600, the population density in Italy, France, and the Netherlands was so high that their agricultural areas could not support them. Every fourth harvest was insufficient. Between 1600 and 1800, twenty-sixths of severe outbreaks of famine and subsequent disease were recorded in France. In Finland, in 1696, every third inhabitant died of starvation.

For several centuries, lack of food destroyed entire populations' mental, social and productive capacities. Robert Fogel, an economist, and nutritionist, said that malnourished people lose weight faster, burn out, and are less efficient, regardless of their lifespan, which was already so low."

*

"Malnutrition was most evident in newborns, who still have particularly severe consequences. During this period, the brain and nervous system develop, resulting in malnutrition which causes different illnesses and more frequent schizophrenia. It was no different in Asia, China, and India.

In the 19th century, the average European was around 165 centimeters tall and weighed about 60 kilograms. Life expectancy was appallingly low. At the height of the British Empire, people lived to be only 40 years old, while working-class people lived just over 20 years, which is about like our Paleolithic ancestors.

After 12 thousand years of civilization, humanity has reached a dead end. A few centuries ago, stunted bodies and malnutrition were a tax on the quickly growing population. In 1804, there were one billion people in the world. In 1927 were already two billion of us. Then the number began to increase significantly. In 1960, it jumped to three billion. At the end of the previous millennium, there were already six billion of us. There are currently more than eight billion of us. How can the population increase from less than two hundred to five billion years if, in the 19th century, starvation due to famine still threatened extinction?"

## The Industrial Revolution

"The industrial revolution brought about the main change. Farmer, in 1837, for growing wheat on one acre, spent 148 hours of work. In 1890, he invested only 37 hours for the same result. With machinery, increasing international integration, the ideology of free trade that took place by rail and sea routes, and new food production and storage technologies, the food industry flourished again.

Globalization has brought about renewed development, and hunger has temporarily stopped. New technologies for canning and freezing meat and other food made it possible to bring food relatively safely and quickly anywhere in the world. This encouraged farmers elsewhere and increasingly involved them in mass production. That has made food a global commodity and not just a necessity for survival.[26]"

The rapidly growing infrastructure marked the beginning of the agricultural revolution. In research centers, experts began to develop new varieties of plants and breeds of animals that grew faster. In the 20s and 30s of the last century, the first corn varieties with giant cones were created, and they grew more densely in the field, which increased the yield per hectare.

Among the most revolutionary discoveries of the 20th century is the Haber-Bosch method for obtaining synthetic ammonia, a difficult-to-access nutrient for plants. At the same time, artificial fertilizers were developed since they could no longer increase the yield sufficiently with manure and plowing. It is estimated that with the help of synthetic fertilizers made from ammonia, produced according to this process, they still feed about a third of the world's population.

By the end of the twentieth century, the modern food system was hailed as the most remarkable achievement of the human species. We have grown more and more grain, meat, fruit, and vegetables than ever, more cheaply than ever, achieving a level of safety, variety, and quality that was unfathomable to previous generations.[27]

## Mechanization Did Not Stop Famine

"In the 60s of the last century, Asia avoided starvation, but the intention to eradicate hunger failed. However, one-seventh of the world's people are still hungry and malnourished. Where hunger has been eradicated, the population is crippled by the effects of modern processed food infused with pesticides—phytopharmaceuticals (FFS), additives, and other chemicals that make food beautiful and attractive, tasty, and long-lasting.

Most people are overweight, and the incidence of chronic and degenerative diseases has reached the highest possible level. Alarming is the data showing an increase in diabetes, cardiovascular disease, autoimmune diseases, cancer, Parkinson's disease, autism, infertility, and others brought about by a stressful lifestyle and unsuitable, dead-processed food. Food is full of calories that are free energy values.[28]"

## Is the Food Industry Really to Blame for Bad Eating Habits?

Everyone should ask themselves this when they step into the mall. Chemicals, produced by mega-corporations for the sensory enhancement of food, today we can find in almost all food: yogurt, processed cheeses, milk with different flavors, drinks that replace milk, carbonated drinks, juices, dried fruits, cereals, snacks, cookies, pastries, candies, chewing gums, meat and meat products, vegetable sauces, pâtés, soups, frozen vegetables and fruits, cans and more could list. In 2016, when I was studying European legislation on nutrition, the "industrial chefs" had more than 4,600 chemicals to recreate flavors and aromas, which give the food a better appearance and color, preservatives for more extended durability, and crispiness additives. Today there are certainly these additives—chemicals already much more.

*

A few years ago, I came across a fascinating book called *Salt, Sugar, Fat: How the Food Giants Hooked Us*, written by a researcher journalist Michael Moss. At that time, I lived in Germany, working in the holistic center of Schokwitz-Heallingcastle. I got a book from my friend Jacqueline Twohie, a New Yorker who went to us for rest and treatment.

Howard Moskowitz is who attracted me the most in this book. Moskowitz deals with market research in the food industry, so I connected with him. Moskowitz is convinced that additives and flavorings are of fundamental importance for developing ready meals and are suitable for health. Thirty years ago, he helped invent the sauce for Spaghetti Prego, which made thousands of Americans happy and was made in 36 versions.

Flavors and aromas can be made in any chemical laboratory. In Slovenia, they are produced by Etol Celje, which acquired a new owner, Frutarom, in 2012. From 2015 to 2016, Frutarom acquired 20 chemical companies worldwide. It operates in 145 countries, where it markets approximately 31 thousands products, and 41 development laboratories operate under its auspices, including the Slovenian Etol—Celje. Officially, Frutarom creates, develops, produces, and markets a wide range of high-quality flavors and aromas and the finest ingredients for the food, beverage, pharmaceutical, food, and cosmetic industries.

Chemicals have flooded the world. Whenever we walk into a store, hundreds of packaged, processed foods await us on the shelves in beautiful packaging, the kind our mind likes because it works based on the five senses. Moskowitz often points out that people do not know what they want and will accept something if feelings and advertisements tell them. His most famous statement is that the mind does not know what the tongue wants. Processed foods destroy our taste buds, like always more salty, sweet, and fat food. All products contain excessive amounts of salt, sugar, and Trans fats that burden the hormonal system, all metabolic organs, the liver, and kidneys. Worth thinking about!

We have ourselves to blame for bad eating habits, not the food industry. Most consumers do not even look at the declarations. If we dig a little deeper, everything is written. Everything is public, accessible to anyone, very transparent, and nothing is hidden because it demands legislation. The problem is that they are harmful additives; so-called E are hidden under different names and tags.

We could say human stupidity knows no bounds. Undoubtedly, it pays more for the food industry to use artificially created versions.

*

Producers of juices and other drinks, such as flavoring strawberries, use only one-fifth of the artificial flavor as if they were natural. The best-known aroma of vanilla is given by a single compound, 4-hydroxy-3-methoxy benzaldehyde, better known as vanillin, which is artificially produced from waste materials in paper production.

Benzaldehyde smells like almonds, and diacetyl tastes like butter, one of the main components from which they can recreate the aroma of pineapple, is chloroform. Since most foods become tasteless during the process, thousands of kilograms of additives are used. Nothing is more accessible and cheaper! Just one gram of aroma is enough to recreate the taste of one kilogram of food.

*

"At the end of the 20th century, Nestlé was the world's largest, somewhat scattered multinational, employing thousands of workers worldwide. For the production of a billion individual food products, such as coffee, cocoa, sugar, milk, oil, wheat, corn, salt, and other ingredients, almost 40 thousand square kilometers of agricultural land are needed, nearly as much as the whole of Switzerland.[29] The earth is worn out, and the plundered planet is collapsing due to consumerist greed and ignorance. Mother Earth is crying."

# Bacteria Create Our Destiny

*"They have no eyes, ears, nose, or teeth. They have no limbs, heart, liver, lungs, or brain. They don't breathe or eat like we do. We can't even see them with the naked eye. They were the first forms of life on the planet and will probably be the last. Why? Because absolutely nothing alive can exist without them, not even you."*
Dr. David Perlmutter (1954), neurogastroenterologist[30]

I am not an analyst, but I am still interested in the benefits of fasting and how it is explained by Western scientific doctrine. Research work refines me and complements my knowledge and experience.

# Christensenella Minute Vs Firmicutes

The mysterious bacterium Christensenella minute was discovered by Prof. Masami Morotomi (Yakult Central Institute for Microbiological Research, Japan). He isolated some microorganisms from a healthy human donor and realized Christensenella had great potential.

Numerous studies have shown that Christensenella is a minor bacteria in individuals with increased physical weight. In 2014, scientists confirmed that overweight people lack this bacteria and are therefore prone to obesity (Goodrich et al., 2014). In the same year, another laboratory discovered that high levels of Christensenella minutes were associated with reduced blood triglyceride concentrations and higher HDL cholesterol. In one of the independent studies, these observations confirmed the same in 2015 (Fu et al., 2015).

Christensenella minute is also associated with diseases such as chronic inflammatory bowel disease (IBD), Crohn's disease, ulcerative colitis (Pascal et al., 2017; Kummen et al., 2017; Zakrzewski et al., 2018), chronic liver disease (Primary Sclerosing Cholangitis—PSC, Kummen et al., 2017), irritable bowel syndrome (Pozuelo et al., 2015) and colon cancer.

## Bacteria Firmicutes

"Ninety percent of the intestinal population is represented by bacteria Firmicutes and Bacteroidetes. The ratio between these two bacteria determines the levels of inflammation and is associated with health problems such as obesity, diabetes, coronary artery disease, and the vascular system. A higher percentage of Firmicutes compared to bacteria Bacteroidetes is strongly associated with inflammation and obesity.

Obesity is related to the production of inflammatory chemicals or cytokines. These molecules mostly come from adipose tissue that acts as an organ and exhausts hormones. It is difficult to imagine being overweight as an inflammatory disease, just as it is hard to imagine dementia and depression being inflammatory.

Firmicutes are exceptionally well adapted to obtain calories from food and increase the absorption of calories. We will likely gain weight if the body absorbs more calories from ingested meals while traveling through the gastrointestinal tract.

A Harvard study found that the Firmicutes bacterium dominates in the intestines of Westerners mainly due to processed and fast food. If Firmicutes dominate the gut, this can have dramatic consequences, as research shows that they regulate human metabolic genes. That means that Firmicutes, which are in the intestines of overweight people, are controlled by genes that do not have a favorable effect on metabolism. They hijack our DNA and create a script that makes our body think it needs to detain the calories.[31]"

In 2015, a study was published in the biomedical journal American Journal of Clinical Nutrition, according to which higher levels of Firmicutes bacteria alter the expression of our genes, which paves the way for obesity, diabetes, and other inflammatory processes in the body. The study also reveals that we can change this by increasing dietary fiber intake, especially plant, and thereby improve the relationship between Firmicutes bacteria and Bacteroidetes.

"In contrast to Firmicutes, Bacteroidetes bacteria specialize in breaking down large plant starches and fibers into smaller molecules of fatty acids that the body can use for energy. Scientists who study this ratio believe that the ratio between F/B became a "biomarker" for obesity. They were confused by the discovery bacterium Christensenella minute. So, it is not all Firmicutes' fault.[32]"

Fat cells do not just store calories. They are in human physiology involved much more than we imagine. If we have more fat as we need it—especially around visceral organs such as the liver, gall kidney, spleen, adrenal glands, kidneys, pancreas, and intestines—our metabolism suffers and does not function optimally.

## Five Days of Fast Already Benefited

The International Journal of Molecular Sciences March 2021 published an extensive study on how even a few days of fasting help manage metabolic and inflammatory diseases and prevent aging-related mechanisms.

"Fasting is gaining popularity, but less is known about the effects of fasting on the gut microbiota and its influence on the epigenetic regulation of critical metabolic enzymes, especially sirtuins (SIRTs). The experiment analyzed the effect of periodic fasting on 51 men's and women's gut microbiota, sirtuin expression, and mitochondrial content. The participants fasted for five days in a row according to the instructions of Dr. Buchinger. Ketogenesis selected mRNA, miRNA, mitochondrial (mt) DNA, and gut composition. Fasting induced a significant switch in metabolism, as indicated by increased expression of ß-hydroxybutyrate (BHB) and pyruvate dehydrogenase kinase isoform 4 (PDK4) in capillary blood. After fasting, the diversity of the gut microbiota increased, and a statistically significant correlation was detected between the expression of the SIRT1 gene and the abundance of Prevotella and Lactobacillus bacteria. The numbers of Christensenella bacteria associated with longevity increased after fasting and inversely correlated with age and index body mass (BMI). That is the first study to show that fasting does not just change the composition of the gut microbiota, making it more diverse but also affects the expression of sirtuins in humans.[33]"

In contrast to a restrictive diet, which usually lasts for a specific time, fasting includes a daily energy intake of up to 250 kcal. The article states that such a supervised fast can last up to three weeks. That is the similar as Panchakarma, or Ayurvedic purification therapy takes place. During fasting, glucose and glycogen stores are depleted, followed by enhanced lipolysis to supply peripheral tissue with free fatty acids, which can later be converted into ketone bodies, mainly liver mitochondria. One of the ketone bodies, ß-hydroxybutyrate (BHB), controls cell signaling and regulates gene expression. In this way, it acts post-transcriptionally actively and reduces the neurological defects associated with aging.

## Who Is SIRT?

"SIRTs are a group of proteins, two of which are essential sirtuin 1 (SIRT1) and sirtuin 3 (SIRT3), which play an essential role in preventing oxidative stress. SIRT1 has been shown to limit oxidative stress in coronary artery endothelial cells exposed to elevated glucose levels. The research was done on diabetic rats. They found that SIRT1 exerted protective effects against diabetes. In lymphocytes, endothelial and stem cells, which had reduced SIRT1, increased oxidative stress causing systemic inflammation.

Partial fasting and fasting in any version favorably alter clinical blood parameters that have already been studied and documented. Besides, they have demonstrated in animals that restrictive diets prolong the activation of SIRT lifetime. The scientists also demonstrated that five days of a reduced diet in humans increases the expression of SIRT1 and SIRT3 compared to control groups of people who did not fast. Partial fasting leads to changes in the microbial composition of the gut. The number of bacteria Christensenella, associated with longevity, increased after fasting. To our knowledge, this is the first study to assess the expression of SIRTs, including their interaction with gut composition, in partially fasted or 250 kcal/day restricted subjects."

*

"SIRT1 is the most intensively studied member of the sirtuin family and is associated with animal longevity. In mammals, seven types of SIRTs (SIRT1-7) have been identified, which are found in different parts of cells and have multiple functions, including DNA repair, cell survival, metabolism, lipid, and glucose homeostasis, resistance to stress, and insulin secretion. The enzyme AMPK (activated protein kinase) and SIRT1 regulate the activities of each other and share many common goals and functions. So AMPK, as SIRTs, promotes mitochondrial biogenesis and function. As a result, they increase the cells' ability to generate adenosine triphosphate, an energy source in various processes, and reduce oxidative stress and other potentially harmful cellular damage.

Sirtuins are also expressed in the gastrointestinal tract. To mice that had no expression—of SIRT3 expression, the intestinal microbiome changed. They showed a higher level of inflammation, and damage to the intestinal epithelium increased. Decreased SIRT expression and decreased gut microbial diversity have been shown to be associated with aging. Dysbiosis—changes the balance between microbes in the gut and is associated with inflammations of the intestinal barrier that trigger diseases such as Crohn's disease, colitis, type 2 diabetes, fatty liver, hepatic steatosis, atherosclerosis, cardiovascular diseases, increased body weight, and aging. The microbiome has been shown to influence the expression of genes that cause epigenetic changes and regulate the activity of receptors that bind short-chain fatty acids (SCFA) to G-proteins. SCFAs are metabolites of the gut microbiota that are produced by the fermentation of dietary fiber.[34]"

# Modern Fasting

*"O SADHU! purify your body in the simple way.
As the seed is within the banyan tree, and within the
seed are the flowers, the fruits, and the shade. So the
germ is within the body, and within that germ is the
body again. The fire, the air, the water, the earth, and
the ether; you cannot have these outside of Him."*
Kabir Sahib (1440-1518)[35]

Today's man has adapted fasting to a great extent. From the Essene writings, we understand rituals are similar to those found in the ancient doctrine of Ayurveda. Ayurvedic purification is gentle and body-friendly. Pure spring water, sun, and air are also the basis of Ayurvedic fasting. That is called Panchakarma, in which a properly selected diet, medicinal-adaptogenic herbs, oils, and other tools are used. "Pancha" means five, and "karma" means action. This way, we try to rebalance the doshas—energies in the body; Vata, Pitta and Kapha.

Panchakarma is a detoxification method, the recipe of which can already be found in the oldest Sanskrit text Charaka Samhita. Indian healers use this method to prolong life to reach the highest goal of life—enlightenment. The method consists of practical steps for eliminating the body's poisons (Sanskrit ama). Among the essential processes in Panchakarma are Nasya, Vamana, Virecana, Raktamoksana and Basti. Water enema only partially clears the large intestine, about 0.5 m long. With ordinary water, enemas do not go that deep. Plus, it has guts follicles in which some impurities and clots stick to the walls large intestine. With Panchakarma treatment and later with continuing with the correct lifestyle and a diet precisely defined and prepared for each individual separately, we maintain the body balance.

## Fasting Reduces Oxidative Stress and Stops Inflammation Processes

Metabolic disorders have increased significantly in developed and developing countries in the last decades. Obesity, type 2 diabetes, hypertension, cardiovascular disease, indigestion, and cancer often contribute to faster aging and higher mortality. Restrictive diets or partial fasting, including time-limited calorie restriction feeding and intermittent fasting, are known to inhibit s age-related diseases and thus prolong life. Lower caloric intake reduces oxidative stress, improves insulin sensitivity, and alters neuroendocrine and sympathetic nervous system function.

# Cancer, Chemotherapy
# and Fasting

*"If you think you can do a thing or think you can't do a thing, you're right."*
Henry Ford, (1863 – 1947), an American industrialist and business magnate[36]

Cancer is the most common and insidious disease in the modern world, and it "sticks" to more and more individuals. Modern medicine has advanced dramatically and has suitable therapies for almost all types of cancer. Some are treated with chemotherapy, others with surgery, and others with cytostatic and biological drugs. It all depends on where the disease has developed, how much it is advanced, what is the body's resistance and, most importantly, how a person accepts a diagnosis that is very unpleasant for many people and worrying.

*

Ayurveda has been talking for thousands of years that all diseases start from an emotional imbalance. Misunderstanding of the soul, or in other words, an imbalance of doshas in the body. The text says that to understand how the body works, we must become conscious of emotions and their role in protecting and maintaining health. We gain this knowledge by understanding the nature of the mind and its function in controlling sense perception. However, the complexity of the human mind we cannot grasp without understanding the soul and the intelligence that guides the mind and life.

*

"Renowned Canadian doctor Dr. Mate Gabor came to similar conclusions. With patients suffering from cancer, the causes, at the end of therapy, were found in unresolved conflicts from the past in the closest family circle, among friends, or at work, constant stress, distorted thought patterns, self-blame, and poor self-image. In other words, they had broken emotions and a 'sick and sad soul'. Of course, genetics, dietary habits, and lifestyle also play a significant role in this—most patients of Dr. Gabor was reported to be lonely and conflicts with loved ones."

*

"When the body is under constant stress, the HHA axis (hypothalamus, pituitary, adrenal glands) unconsciously causes the secretion of two vital dangerous hormones, cortisol and adrenaline. They damage the adrenal gland, an endocrine gland vital for producing other hormones to keep our body functioning optimally and in balance. When this balance is disturbed, it forms in the body chaos—disorder. That is reflected differently in each individual. Also, each individual solves problems differently. Some become anxious, and others are in a constant spasm of anger and aggression. Others fall into inactivity and depression.[37]"

In addition to the constant emotional overload, there is another thing to consider environmental factors. In 1967, a professor, an excellent scientist, and one of the first cell biologists to master the art of cloning stem cells, Irving William Konigsberg (1923-2008), told a historical fact: "When cells grown in a cellular structure are sick, it is necessary to first look for the causes in the environment, in which the cell is, but not in the cell itself."

Scientists who rely on Darwinism continue to neglect environmental factors. They overemphasize the nature of genetic determinism—the belief that genes control biology. That wrong belief has changed the way we think about our lives. If we believe that genes control our lives and cannot influence them, we can see ourselves as victims of inherited traits, saying that as my mother had cancer, so will I. In case of inappropriate diet, poor lifestyle, emotional instability, and constant stress, this will happen because that is our belief.

Some scientific interpretations of single gene errors affect less than two percent of the population. Diseases such as diabetes, heart disease, and cancer are not caused by a single gene but by the complex interaction of several genes and environmental factors.

*

"Dr. Ernam Mayer, Professor of Medicine, Physiology, and Psychiatry, wrote about his findings regarding the unbalanced Western diet. An extensive report in a UCLA (University of California, Los Angeles) press release: "Knowing that signals travel from the gut to the brain and that they can influence through changes in diet will lead to more extensive research. We will search for new strategies to prevent and treat digestive, mental, and neurological disorders. Exist studies of what we eat can change the composition and products of the intestinal flora. Mainly, people who eat a lot of vegetables and fiber have a different composition of the microbiota or the intestinal environment than people who eat a more typical Western diet high in fat and carbohydrates. Now we know that it affects not just metabolism, but also brain functions.[38]"

The fact that changes in our intestines affect how the brain responds to our emotions is impressive and, for humanity, crucial information. It means everything that we consume, with what we feed the gut microbiome, the bacteria that live there, affects the functioning of our brain.

## Ayurveda and Prakriti

In elementary school, we were told that the Earth was created with a big bang. With the presence of fire, dust particles, water, air, and space, are five elements condensed into the Earth, on which the first living things were bacteria, viruses, and unicellular organisms. Ayurveda also talks about this, but the terminology is slightly different. It talks that all five elements are present at birth in our body. The state of birth is called Prakriti. I will describe it in a short, simple way all three doshas—energies are made up of the same five elements: fire, water, earth, air, and ether (space).

The dosha Vata is a composite of air and ether. Working with the heart is the most sensitive, emotional, subtle, and intuitive. Dosha Vata is inclined to anxiety and fear. She hides from problems and waits until the storm passes or finds a way to escape them. She usually finds solace in food, alcohol, or drugs. The seat of the dosha Vata is in the large intestines, and when she is out of balance is prone to constipation, bloating, and gasses.

Dosha Pitta is composed of fire and water. Her seat is the small intestine and the liver. Pitta is rational. She works with logos, mind, and ego. Problems are often a real challenge for a dosha Pitta. When she is out of balance is bilious and bursts into impatience, anger, and jealousy. In this case, the gastrointestinal system is affected—liver, ulcers on the stomach, increased acid, reflux, stomach ulcers, diverticula, headaches, high blood cholesterol, skin problems, and migraines.

The dosha Kapha consists of water and Earth. This person is compassionate and warm-hearted and keeps things inside, hoping everything will work. The seat of the Kapha is in the stomach. It is responsible for the lymphatic system. When her balance is disturbed, she is subject to respiratory diseases, such as asthma, flu, angina, virus, and pneumonia, because excess accumulates on mucus. Like the dosha Vata, it does not like fire due to its lack of avoiding conflicts. When there is out of balance often leads to excessive eating and buying unnecessary material goods. This person solves problems more rationally. It takes time and does well. Kapha thinks about how she will deal with problems and later solves them calmly.

All three doshas are in each of us but different proportions. The ratio of doshas at birth is called Prakriti. That depends on the condition of our parents at the time of conception, their lifestyle style, dietary habits, and genetics.

If we have the most exposed gene in our genetic record, which determines that we can get cancer, we will we got this because we believe in it. Those are our beliefs, and so we are thinking. Emotions create our thoughts, and thoughts create actions. When emotions are affected, the function of the HHA axis does not function properly. However, this is, of course, not the reason we get cancer. The disease manifests slowly; it usually takes years before a particular imbalance manifests itself. We are warned about other illnesses before that, which we mostly ignore. We usually go to a doctor who prescribes medicine, and we stick a patch on the wound, which has a short shelf life and unpleasant side effects.

Ayurveda recommends releasing our emotions into the ether (space). In the West, this means seeing a therapist with whom we can talk honestly.

Unfortunately, there are not enough experts, so we usually get Band-Aids in the form of antidepressants, psychotics, sleeping pills, antirheumatic drugs, and other drugs that suppress emotions and pain.

## Cancer—A Disease of Emotions and Unresolved Conflicts from the Past

When the worst comes, things change drastically. Storms in the head, anxiety, and fear are present in anyone who faces a cancer diagnosis. A few of my patients had to go through a dark history of chemotherapy. That is when another door usually opens. The door to self-knowledge, who we are, where we are going, and our purpose on this planet. It is a specific blueprint given to us at birth. Old souls do not incarnate into the next life, they do their thing here mission, and they understand why the disease befell them. They accept it as dignified because they know they will survive and learn much from the story. Others who do not respect Mother Earth do not believe in creation, and pure consciousness insists on their own. Some survive, but the most "stubborn" have to leave the planet and be reborn—reincarnated so they can improve their story and complete it in their next life. Some souls are so wounded that when they are diagnosed with cancer, they let their lives go, do not fight back, and wait in peace to leave.

Chemotherapy is not only poison for cancer cells but also everyone else. The most potent and persistent are not afraid of cancer and endure chemotherapy, but it is not easy for anyone. How much misery and suffering were experienced knows only those who experienced it. Residues of drugs and chemotherapy remain in the body and "nest" in fatty tissue and intestines. Usually, people lose hair, and nails, gain weight, have muscle aches and fullness of poisoned lymph that stagnates in the body, suffer from headaches, and insomnia, feel psychological helplessness and are tormented by anxiety and depression. However, they win because they believe in the light of life.

# Cleaning Up the Aftermath of Medicines and Chemotherapy

*"How glorious is the gift of a friend, who does not hide his pain from you! Have you seen the oaks? With you, they are powerful, firm, always speaking the same words, upright. Have you seen the oaks? In a storm? Have you seen the grass? They are delicate and fragile with you, be careful, because you can step on them! Have you seen the grass? In a storm?"*
Boro Leban, January 2020[39]

Šobec is small camping near mountain resort Bled in Slovenia. I camped there last summer while writing the book. I met a wonderful couple in their mature years. A friendly neighbor helped me set up the tent. With our neighbors, we every day exchanged a few kind words. I'm like a nomad who likes to move around. In addition to food and other things, I always carry my first book *Fasting, The Seed of Health*. I was sorry when the two neighbors left because they were wonderfully calm and compassionate This was felt in their closeness, love, devotion and belonging. I gave them a book out of gratitude. The gentleman flipped through it, read a few lines and said he needed this book. When I asked him why, he said, "Because I have my first chemo tomorrow. And then I'm going to need your help to clean this mess out of my body."

We talked for quite some time, and I felt his strength, desire for life, light in his heart, positive attitude, and love. He will live a long time, an inner voice told me. See you after chemotherapy! Good luck, Matjaž.

*

Chemotherapy and other synthetic drugs leave unwanted effects on the body, bind to fat tissue and intestines, and wait for the immune system to weaken. If we do not have healthy bacteria, we do not have an "army" to fight the microbes. Harmful bacteria enter our bodies with poor hygiene daily through the air, water, and processed food. That is how new diseases arise, mainly unrelated to the disease we have overcome. Many people buy probiotics hoping to strengthen their gut. However, the recommended quantities indicated on the packaging are often misleading. People have a destroyed intestinal flora due to unhealthy, fast, pre-prepared food, canned food, and salty and sweet snacks. We always have a natural and non-invasive solution, but we often do not notice what we have in front of our eyes. Just as the Little Prince says, "The essence is invisible to the eyes."

# Testimonies

### Mateja Dermastja (45)

My name is Mateja Dermastja, and I am 45 years old. I received in January 2020 a phone call from the doctor: "I have your biopsy results. Please contact me today and do not drive alone. Let someone drive you!" I have already been sitting in front of the doctor for an hour. "You must go to the Oncology Institute tomorrow, so it will not be too late!" With all the confusion in my head, I could barely hear the doctor's voice: "The result is positive. You have cancer."

I was barely aware of the situation. Tumor and lymph nodes were removed. After three weeks, both wounds became severely inflamed. After the puncture,

I was given antibiotics, which I took for fifteen days. Chemotherapy followed, but I did not tolerate it well. The doctor put me on painkillers because of the severe pain, and my blood sugar went up a lot. They set up a diagnosis of diabetes and introduced insulin injections. Every time I passed a stool, I bled profusely and had terrible pain that started problems with inflammation near the nails. Four operations followed (nail removal), and a ten-day course of antibiotics after each operation. The hand started to swell a lot—diagnosed with lymphedema. After completion of chemotherapy, radiation followed. It was not without complications here either, and she followed a ten-day course of antibiotics again. The treatment then continued with biological drugs.

After a good year of treatment, I got the last application of biological medicines. My body was affected by all the drugs, anesthetics, and antibiotics. I felt fear about how to proceed. Medical treatment was ending, but I could barely stand on my feet. I was ultimate without energy, strength, and will. I felt that every cell in my body was burning. My veins run poison, not blood. The burning sensation in my head was so intense that I did not sleep all night. I am still with every bowel movement bleeding and in pain. Severe edema of the right hand, pain in my hand, and reduced mobility were the final straw when I realized that I had to change something radically because I won't be able to continue like this. In addition to all the physical problems that plagued me, I was also eaten away by the fact that my current way of life brought me to the disease. If I want to stay healthy, I have to change my lifestyle and diet to make sure my cancer doesn't come back. Yes, that is it, but how?

I started looking for solutions. What kind of therapy should I choose, what to eat…? I had a million questions that I did not have answers to. I only knew I needed a therapist, a mentor whom I could trust, who would care about my problems, with whom I would feel safe.

I read an article about Bilka Baloh in a magazine. On the Internet, I immediately read in detail everything that Google offered under her name. On her website, I saw she also wrote a book, *Fasting, The Seed of Health*. I ordered it, and when I got it, I knew behind is a person with a big heart and knowledge. She wrote a dedication in the book. When the book arrived, a heart and a star were drawn on the cardboard box (I still keep that box today). That was what touched my heart. I devoured the knowledge from the book and found myself in what was written. I called Bilka and made an appointment for a consultation.

During the introductory meeting, Bilka listens carefully to me about my problems. Explained how I feel and that I need fasting to "reset" the body, cleanse it of toxins, and start eating according to my constitution. I immediately felt that Bilka was someone I could completely trust and surrender to. She has a lot of knowledge and experience, and, more importantly, she does her work with heart and warmth.

We agreed to start fasting immediately after the last application of biological drugs. There were three more weeks until the last therapy. During this time, I studied the protocol Bilka put together exclusively for me and my problems. I had time, bought everything I needed, and could not wait for the day we decided to begin fasting.

On the first day, I had severe headaches and was exhausted and without energy. If I did not have Bilka by my side cheering me on, I would give up immediately. The headache subsided on the third day, but I was still there without energy and exhausted. I was only up for so long to make the morning protocol, prepare teas and soups, meditate, and go for a walk. I spent the rest of the day in bed and overslept. There were days when I could not read books or even write a diary. We spoke with Bilka every day, even several times a day. I needed to report my feelings because I had been on insulin before. She adjusted the protocol on the fly to make me feel better.

The eighteenth day was the worst, literally hellish. When I got up in the morning, I thought that I would not last an hour more and would fall to the ground and never recover. I called Bilka, who was, as always, full of love and compassion. Without words or reproaches, she told me I could stop if I could not take it anymore, even though we had planned a twenty-one-day fast. Her warmth and love gave me incredible strength to continue fasting even in the most difficult moment for me.

Two hours after our conversation, I experienced something incredible. A wave of powerful, unknown energy washed over me, washed away all my weight. From that moment on, I was reborn and full of energy. I felt super energetic and light for the last three days of the fast. In addition to invaluable knowledge, Bilka also has warmth and love, which I needed in addition to knowledge.

After fasting, I started eating according to Bilka's protocol, which she compiled exclusively for me and my constitution. That is how I eat even now, a few months after fasting. Although it is not always easy, I persevere and live a new lifestyle. The pain is gone, and I no longer have blood in my bowel movements. I do not need insulin anymore, the burning sensation in my body and head has disappeared, and the lymphedema has decreased by 50 percent. The pain in my arm is still there, but I know it will go away. As Bilka says, nothing happens overnight, but slowly everything. I know that this was not my last fast, and I will perform all the following ones under Bilka's auspices.

Bilka, thank you for all the knowledge and support on my thorny paths!

Mateja Dermastja, Rakek, 3 July 2021

*

## Saša Gerčar (56)

I got 'burnt out'. A few years ago, long-term chronic stress strongly affected my immune system and my health. At that time, I had so many problems that it would be too much to describe and thickened Bilka's book, so let me only mention the final balance of years of turning a blind eye to reality, which I still feel today. I lost almost half of my teeth. I also lost all my hair during the traumatic period of two years. I have been walking around the world entirely bareheaded for eight years now. I also destroyed my thyroid, so I start each day with three tiny pills that balance my thyroid hormones. And still, stress sticks to me faster than a wasp to honey. I dug myself out of this black hole for a few years, somehow crawled out, and lived a reasonably normal life in strange, corona-tinged times.

That late autumn, however, my strength was waning. What sounded like a friendly chat a few months ago has become nothing more than a rant. What was once a happy walk with the dog became an hour, freezing and moving through muddy meadows. Not to mention the delicious, home-baked cookies that were delicious with coffee in the spring, but just something that sticks to my ass in October. The number on the scale was approaching three digits, and I was everything more depressed. I added a new lifelong dose of chemistry to the hormone pills—pills to reduce stomach acid.

In such an autumnal melancholic, almost depressed state, I listened to a colleague who decided to fast. Not for some diet, for absolute fasting, where you eat practically nothing, actually 'you are starving'. However, the enema is such a stunt. After three weeks of starvation, my colleague was full of goodwill and energy, so I "googled" a little and already sent a message to Bilka Baloh, who guided my colleague through fasting. As I read online, she wrote a book about fasting. Moreover, during the "hungry days", many people were safely transported under her supervision. Bilka and I quickly exchanged ideas. She prepared a program for a 14-day fast. I was hoping for 21 but quietly said I would be the winner after ten.

The preparations were almost worse than the fasting. I had to get a list of organic vegetables, a juicer, sesame oil, and brushes for this and that part of the body. Then to the library to get books for my three-week 'vacation'. I decided to be unemployed, without radio and television. I removed all creams and lipsticks from the shelves and nail polish; if I had hair, I would let it go gray during this time. I also got rid of social network applications. Withdrawn, I took them from the first page of the phone and closed them in a special drawer with a label UNTOUCHABLE.

My expectations? Ah, what do I know? I jumped into it quite a bit spontaneously. Although they say that fasting should not be an excuse to lose weight, I secretly wanted to lose a few extra kilos. I needed that kick in the ass that would give me the impetus to improve my eating habits.

Reflux and too much acid were the problems that led me to persistently "pop" the previously mentioned pills, which I desperately wanted to get rid of them. The way my friend felt better and better again during fasting was the idea that I would try too. To get rid of stubborn white plaques that have been covering the entire surface of my tongue for several years due to the pills I have been using. What is more, I would be happy if I could get rid of the asymmetrical red spot on my décolleté, which the dermatologist declared "worth watching" months ago.

I grabbed the devil by the horns, and one Monday in November, I started fasting. I struggled with each day separately. Every day was a new challenge, a new step, and I loudly congratulated myself on a successful breakthrough every evening.

There were days when the "sun shone" and days when it 'poured like a bucket'. There were days full of hope and days when I would have thrown the shotgun into the corn and emptied the box of vanilla ice cream.

I was most afraid of fear. When I started to fear myself, the pimple that appeared on my lower left buttock could also destroy me. There were quite a few such days during the fast. When you only drink slightly yellow water boiled with vegetables for nineteen days, and a bunch of something falls into the toilet bowl during an enema, a man of my kind is horrified. Or you have not drunk anything red for the tenth day; on the other hand, red water is still flowing after the enema. Then you get a scenario that is worse than the content of the movie Jaws or Bridge on the River Kwai. The acid disturbed my sleep. Instead of the expected rapid improvement, I suffered severely for some time during the fast.

A week after the last day of fasting, I only ate boiled rice. Step by step, the situation improved. I lost 13 kilograms and three more in the following ten months during the fast. Ten months later, I maintained my weight with no reflux, and I feel excellent. Today I am reflux-free and off antacids, the tongue is much pinker, and the spot on the cleavage is barely noticeable.

I would give up on the first major problem. I would not have succeeded without Bilka. We joked every day and even saw each other often. She kindly helped me get over all the "pimples on my butt" and the idea of bleeding with an expert explanation. Together, we got through those twenty-one days, the reflux that was tearing me up, the pain in my spine, my legs, the coating on my tongue, the freckles on my cleavage, and the low energy.

Saša Gerčar, Ljubljana, 1 August 2022

*

## Elke Max Stopper (48)

I am Elke, 48 years old, mother of two grown sons. At the age of 31, I overcame ovarian cancer with the help of official medicine because I had not yet used alternative methods and did not know enough about this type of treatment. Currently, I am facing a cancer diagnosis for the second time in my life. I didn't know enough. I had an operation—removal of the left ovary and fallopian tube and three cycles of chemotherapy. My child was still small, and I didn't even dare to experiment and rely on "alternative" methods. The decision then fell as it did. I have no regrets because cancer has not recurred in all these years. But from then on, I was no longer the same as before the treatment, as the chemotherapy left consequences on my body. The white blood cell count never came back to normal, so my immune system didn't work as it used to, either.

After completing the treatment, I got the drive and motivation to change something in my life. I always regretted that I didn't finish college and thus secure a better future for myself. I turned my life upside down. With two small children and a job, I enrolled in college. As long as I studied and worked on myself, on changes, I felt much fulfilled. I started reading motivational books, and researching which way of eating would be the most suitable for me, and with this, I gained a broader view of what is needed for health—not only physically but also emotionally, spiritually, and psychologically.

A few years later, I developed thyroid inflammation and thyroid nodules. I was given extremely strong medicines, which, despite everything, did not guarantee a cure. I was still waiting for treatment with radioactive iodine. This time I decided to get involved in the entire treatment process and not just wait for what the doctors will do for me. After the literature I read, I was most convinced by fasting, so I decided to try this option first and thus help the body to heal itself. I was scared about the nodules—what if they were too malignant? Just because of the fear of cancer recurrence, I easily decide to give up food for a while and consume only fruit and vegetable juices.

I started fasting myself because, at that time, I didn't know people who would deal with it and take me through this 'journey'. Throughout the fast, I was moving and had an incredible amount of energy, which continued to increase. I did not feel sick. But I was skeptical if I would last because good food means a lot to me. I began without expectations. I wanted to test for myself if it really work. I was just worried about how I would go without food for so long. Since I felt very good from the start, it motivated me to persevere easily.

And it was worth it. After completing the twenty-one-day fast, the drugs were discontinued, as the thyroid hormones returned to normal. I did not need a radioiodine test or surgery, and that was the end of the treatment. In addition, I was proud that I had achieved my goal and survived without any major problems.

I began to realize that I was obviously doing something very wrong because I always do get sick again. I followed the right path for a long time until I started to feel better, and everything was fine with me again. After that, I had no major problems but slipped back into an unhealthy lifestyle: bad food, a lot of meat, fast food, bread, and no movement in the fresh air. It was much easier to live according to an old, familiar pattern than to start changing your habits.

However, I was aware even then that this method had gotten me sick in the past, and it was only a matter of time before I got the warning again. Still, I wasn't strong enough to change my eating habits. I looked for answers in the spiritual world, which required me to actively participate in the healing process, but it was an effort for me. With this way of life, I quickly "noticed" that my body has no way to cleanse itself from large amounts of unhealthy food. Every illness drove me to research what is the right and better way of life.

A few years later, cysts were discovered on my breasts and a puncture was performed. Luckily, it was nothing serious, but I took it as a warning to take action before something worse developed. I decided to fast again but in a group. I spent the first twelve days fasting on my own and then "did" the remaining nine days in the group.

But this time, it wasn't so easy—I didn't have the motivation, but I was just waiting for the last day. Because I had to pay the reservation for group fasting, it encouraged me to start alone and finish with a group. After twenty-one days, the cysts did not disappear, but the formation disappeared, which the doctors had to monitor, as there was a risk that they would turn malignant.

Last October, however, I was diagnosed with cancer again, this time for a second type and second location—melanoma on the choroid of the left eye. The diagnosis honestly shook me. But I already, before the treatment, made a decision in the hospital that I would start fasting again, this time for forty-two days. I was a little scared because forty-two days seemed like an eternity. I wasn't physically weak, but mentally I was in a lot of pain before I accepted the situation I found myself in again. I did not dare to fast myself this time to tackle. That's why I was looking for a qualified person.

On the same day, a web search revealed an article about Bilka Baloh. Her approach convinced me, and I felt that she was the one I was looking for. I contacted her and signed up for the appointment. Bilka welcomed me extremely kindly, told me some basics about Ayurveda, and then we focused on fasting. I have to say this was the time that it went worse than before because I was mentally extremely weak, sad, and scared. Having a history of severe acid problems, I took heartburn medicine to calm the stomach acid. The problem lasted for the first fourteen days of the fast. I felt like I had a fire in my stomach.

On the fifteenth day, I woke up without the burning pain in my stomach, but then it stopped completely. Today is the thirty-second day of the fast. It's only been a month, but I'm feeling much better. Bilka supported me every day. When I needed her, she helped me with answers, warmth, and understanding.

She was great support and motivation all the time. Every piece of her advice and every conversation comforted me again and again, and I persevered and continued. A few times during the fast, I thought that I could not do more. And without Bilka, I would have probably stopped because I sometimes felt sick because I drank much less than recommended.

With every bad feeling, I began to doubt whether I was on the right path. Bilka comforted me again and again and thus gave me the impetus to continue, and the fear disappeared. A sense of security, a sense that I am not alone in this. Yes, under Bilka's guidance, I devoted myself to the correct way of eating even after the end of the fast. I got the feeling that this time I would get all the necessary knowledge to stay on the "right" path.

Has this fast done anything to shrink the tumor? At this point, I don't know because the control after eye surgery is waiting for me in a fortnight. However, it definitely solved the problem with excess stomach acid, which I can say from my own feeling.

So I passed the physical part, but now I have to fix my mental and spiritual state. I walk up to Bilka again, who emphasizes the benefits of meditation. I have already ticked off the diet correctly because Bilka prepared a list for me of what I can eat for the first two weeks after the end of the fast, so I got precise instructions, not just the sentence: "Now start eating healthy"! I am aware that I still have a long way to go before I conquer and deepen my knowledge of alternative healing methods. This time I will dedicate myself even more to my spiritual path.

I am immensely grateful to Bilka Baloh for having me help to stay on the right path and gave her knowledge and experience unselfishly shared with me.

—Elke Maks Stoper, Bresternica, December 2021

# Les Calories for Vital Life

*"If you want the truth, I'll tell you the truth: Listen to the
secret sound, the real sound, which is inside you."*
Kabir Sahib (1440-1518)[40]

## Too Many Calories Burden the Body

While writing the book, I spent a few days with my dog
at the seaside. Since Sophia Gea was still a puppy, the
movements were intended for her needs. I'm not a
person who goes to the sea at the peak of the season.
Crowds and negative vibes bother me if there are too
many people in the same place. Nevertheless, I went
on a sort of working vacation to Poreč. The beautiful

seaside resort is located in Istria, Croatia. As usual, I brought most of the food with me. From time to time, I went to the marketplace in Poreč to get fruit and vegetables.

I was surprised by the consumers and the selection of local restaurants. Involuntarily and probably due to professional deformity—my gaze was escaping to people's shopping baskets and to plates that were already full of hearty meals at ten in the morning. Evenings were spent walking to the nearby cape, from where the path took me to the city's center. There are plates in restaurants full of all kinds of "goodies", mainly meat, fish, fries, and other fried foods—too big portions at the wrong time. In the evening, the pancreas, our "factory" for producing enzymes, which processes the food we eat, no longer works optimally. Late dinners stay in the stomach and rot. Due to putrefaction and fermentation, chemical processes are triggered that feed the bad bacteria that acidify the blood. In the evening, we feed pathogenic, body-threatening bacteria that lower the immune system.

I thought about what our metabolic and digestive systems have to go through in order for humans to satisfy their nutritional needs. As well as others: the need for bakery products, desserts, ice cream, snacks, as well as clothes, and shoes. Not to mention all the other junk. I call unnecessary spending of money garbage.

Consumerism can only thrive if we feel disconnected and yearn to fill the emptiness we fill by spending, and in doing so, we try to connect with the whole. We try to fill the emptiness inside us with food, drink, alcohol, drugs, gambling, and unnecessary purchases. Our most essential need that defines feeding is hunger, and so we consumers distance ourselves from ourselves with our constant desire for food.

## Intermittent Fasting

Today, many people use the so-called "trendy" of intermittent fasting 16 to 8, during which the process of autophagy is triggered. We are supposed to "fast" for sixteen hours every day, including sleep time. All meals should be eaten within eight hours. So if the last meal is eaten at 6 p.m., we can start eating the next day at 10 a.m. For most people, this form of intermittent fasting is also the easiest, as it is not a question of limiting caloric intake, only of a different distribution of meals.

Opinions of nutritionists about this are divided. Some are enthused about intermittent fasting, and others warn that it is a waste of weight simply due to water loss, which is partially true. People usually gain the pounds back as soon as they return to their old eating habits. Opponents of intermittent fasting also point out that it is a form of eating that deviates from a balanced diet and an excuse to overeat after the mentioned period.

Intermittent fasting may have been unknowingly taken from Ayurveda. Ayurveda advocates the theory that the last meal should be consumed no later than 4 p.m. and the next at 8 a.m., which is nothing more than an intermittent fast. According to Ayurveda, breakfast is light, no later than 8:00 a.m., and the main meal, lunch, should be when the digestive fire—Agni, is the strongest, between 11:00 a.m. and 1:00 p.m., and dinner between 4:00 p.m. and 6:00 p.m.

The quantities of food and medicinal herbs in Ayurveda are precisely determined according to Prakriti, taking into account Vikriti—the current state, that is, the state to which the balance in the body is disturbed. Based on this, a cleansing program—Panchakarma is prescribed, diet, adaptogenic herbs, yoga, and meditation to balance Vikriti with Prakriti. Then order or balance reigns in the body.

**Autophagy**

Yoshinori Osumi, a Japanese cell biologist, is known for his research into the cellular process of 'recycling'. His work bore fruit in 1990 when he revealed the molecular mechanisms that opened many possibilities for using autophagy for clinical purposes. In 2016, he received the Nobel Prize for his discoveries about autophagy. Autophagy removes damaged cells or cell organelles and proteins, making room for new ones.

Autophagy is also called cytoplasmic or cell death, which is the process of breaking down the cell's own components with the help of lysosomes, which the cell can reuse and thereby obtain the necessary nutrients. Autophagy is a precisely regulated process that plays an important role during cell growth and in maintaining the cellular balance between synthesis and degradation processes. Evolutionarily speaking, the process evolved as a response to starvation for cellular survival under specific conditions.

Modern fasting does not starve the body but cleanses it with the help of cleansing teas, vegetable juices, soups, medicinal herbs, warm water, and mandatory enemas. This type of fasting is safe, as toxins that have accumulated in the body are eliminated from the body, and at the same time, we get the support of the blood.

# Therapeutic Fasting

*For most people are thoroughly convinced that the more they eat, the better they are nourished. Of course, it is not true. One is often much better nourished if one eats less, because then one does not poison oneself.*
Rudolf Steiner (1861-1925), Austrian philosopher, poet and writer[41]

In contrast to hedonism, the word fasting has a negative, unfriendly connotation for many people, but the opposite is true. Fasting transforms from worse to better, eliminates poisons, dead cells, and mucus, and removes parasites and heavy metals with suitable preparations and accessories.

Fasting and cleansing the body are necessary and suitable for today's time and life because we live in an environment full of poisons that enter our body through food, drink, air, cleaners, cosmetics, and clothes. The decision to gather enough strength and courage for the first fast is quite difficult for someone. Fasting affects not only the physical body but also the emotions. That is why it is good to equip yourself beforehand with the knowledge and tools to make your first fast, gentle, friendly, and enjoyable. Order, discipline, and perseverance help us to establish harmony between mind, body, and spirit.

We usually change our eating habits and therapeutic detox when we have reached the breaking point, and we feel so bad that we have no other choice. Cleansing the body is the last hint from creation that we must take the reins of health into our own hands. The decision is the most important. It is crucial for those who are fasting for the first time. Before fasting, the body should be well prepared. What is more, it has to be an experience you need and want. A few days before the fast started, we prepared the body by eating warm and liquid food. Vegetable soups, steamed vegetables, kitchari, pureed vegetables, and fruits are suitable for our constitution. At least a week before the start, excluding meat, milk, gluten, and alcohol from the diet and tobacco is necessary.

According to Vedic dietetics, meat affects Tamas and Rajas. Tamas is the state of consciousness in which interno mechanisms are involved, and Rajas increase fire and egocentric mechanisms. The immune system perceives meat as aggression and irritability increase. Eating tamasic food slows down rehabilitation processes in the body. Tamas and Rajas foods and drinks are meat, fish, garlic, mushrooms, alcohol, and all processed and microwaved foods.

I adapted the therapeutic fasts according to Ayurvedic principles for modern people. I prepare a fasting protocol separately for each individual. Fasting should be gentle, non-aggressive for the body, but above all, safe. People can use the protocol at any time in the future and can fast at home under the supervision of an experienced person.

During the fast, the body is cleansed and renewed, and the skin is tightened, but at the same time, it becomes soft, velvety, and shiny. The gut microbiome cleans the dirt and bad bacteria that are there with the right enemas. With carrying the protocol and schedule, we change and rejuvenate day by day. If it is being done for the first time, it makes sense to take your time for it. It is important to have a mentor to guide you safely through this miraculous transformation.

## We Detoxify Ourselves Like Onion Peels

Toxins from the food we eat last will be the first to leave our body. We only feel hunger for the first few days until the stomach shrinks. The stomach is a muscle and shrinks to the size of a clenched fist during fasting. This is its natural size. The first three days are, therefore, somewhat uncomfortable. After three days, triglycerides begin to be secreted from the liver. These are simple fats that accumulate in the liver and make it difficult for it to function properly. In the case of elevated triglycerides (above 2.3 mmol/l), it is necessary to reduce body weight. Otherwise, diabetes may occur.

After just a few days of fasting, the body's intelligence begins to be balanced, and our strength is restored. When the body starts to really detox, it shows how acidified we are and how many toxins have accumulated in our body. The body then tackles the poisoned lymph. Women call it cellulitis or orange skin. Detoxification is different for each individual—well, that's why we keep in touch during the process. When chemicals, drugs, phytopharmaceuticals, and various additives from industrially processed food, which are bound to fat tissue, return to the bloodstream, they can cause discomforts such as headache, low blood pressure, high acidity, muscle pain, occasional insomnia or back pain. When we are without energy and feel bad during fasting, it means that there are many toxins in the blood that are leaving our bodies. Therefore, it is necessary to drink a lot of warm water and herbal teas so that the toxins are flushed out as soon as possible.

We always drink water and tea warm so that toxins can be eliminated more easily and quickly. If we drink cold water, we shock the fat cells. These shrinks, and instead of the toxins accumulated in the lymph floating away, they remain there, stopping the detoxification process.

It is appropriate to do the first fast in peace so that we have time for ourselves, our bodies, and our thoughts. We spend as much time as possible in silence. During fasting, we do not burden the body with major physical efforts, as the internal organs work at half capacity. That's why I recommend walking, yoga, meditation, breathing, and relaxation exercises during fasting. The body must rest as much as possible, and it must be caressed both from the inside and the outside. Fasting also gives us enough time to think about our eating habits in the future.

## Therapeutic Fasting Retreats

For the first fast to really bear fruit, it makes sense to do it in a group. Retreating to nature, away from the everyday hustle and bustle, low vibrations, and stress, which cripples our lives, helps us to purify the organs in peace and revitalize them. At the same time, we have the opportunity to devote ourselves exclusively to our body, mind, and spirit. The group connects and supports each other. Therefore fasting is easier to perform. Therapeutic retreat—that bears the name *Fasting, The Seed of Health*, is designed holistically and is adapted for each participant individually, according to his constitution and psychophysical capabilities.

We take up to six to eight participants in a group. Fasting and activities are tailored to the readiness and needs of individuals. When necessary, we change them daily. We are housed in the natural environment.

Fasting is a spiritual journey, so we also perform a one-day silence, meditate, perform Hatha yoga, practice conscious breathing—Pranayama, indulge in a sound bath, sauna, and listen to lectures on the topic healthy and balanced diet, which is determined according to the constitution of each individual, we go for long walks, we are in contact with nature and negative ions that eliminate harmful free radicals healthy cells.

The fast lasts seven days. Sometimes, participants want to move on fast for ten days or more. Establishing and regulating digestion after fasting is often a true art, as transitioning to dense food must be body-friendly and gentle. Healthy bacteria, the protagonists of the immune system, must also be colonized in the gut microbiome. That's why we have a special lecture on how to prepare healthy meals after fasting so as not to burden the pancreas, duodenum, gall bladder, spleen, and small and large intestines.

The body is still being cleansed even after the end of the fast when we start introducing gentle and non-aggressive meals adapted to the constitution of the individual.

At the end of the fast, each participant receives a nutrition protocol for the next three months. This is food that does not cause inflammatory processes in the body and strengthens the gut microbiome and, consequently, the immune system.

Body and mind are revitalized, and you go home lighter, full of energy, and richer for an unforgettable experience that it reflects on a physical, emotional, intellectual, and spiritual level.

# The Future Is in Plant-Based Diet

*"Animals are my friends ... and I don't eat my friends. I choose not to make a graveyard of my body with the rotting corpses of dead animals."*
George Bernard Shaw (1856-1950) Irish playwright, Nobel laureate[42]

There is no longer any doubt that fasting is healing, and simultaneous meditation, which is introduced gradually, is self-healing of mind and body. Healthy eating habits are a real puzzle these days.

As I already mentioned, food bought in shopping centers is processed and "enriched" with various additives. Fruits and vegetables are full of phytopharmaceuticals that disrupt the functioning of the endocrine system. Especially meat, meat products, milk, and dairy products are against a healthy way of eating, as they acidify the blood and damage the microbiome.

Five years ago, I read the book The World Peace Diet, written by Will Tuttle. I immediately contacted him and thanked him for such advanced work that has enriched the knowledge of millions of people around the world. Last summer, we reconnected and shared some helpful information about long-term meat-free eating.

## Let's Raise Awareness with Ecology Plant Diet

In our society, the values of the old animal husbandry cultures still apply. We have also preserved their main ritual—eating animals that we treat as objects. If we want to evolve and reach a more spiritually mature level of understanding and life and create a social order in which there will be more justice, peace, freedom, health, mental health, prosperity, and happiness, we must stop treating animals as food items.

The livestock culture we were born into planted the seeds of competitiveness, arrogance, restlessness, greed, greed, fear, and disconnection in us. When we become aware of the consequences of our dietary choices and begin to consciously consume plant-based foods, thereby ceasing to participate in the dominance of the animal world, which lowers consciousness, the ability to connect will also develop and strengthen.

## Overlooked Pythagoras' Message to the World

As previously described, some of the world's greatest thinkers, philosophers, mathematicians, and anthropologists advocated meatless food, food not soiled with blood. Some enthusiastically accepted and applied his ideas, but the main point was overlooked. The Western world has appropriated it and denied its knowledge and true mission. Today, Pythagoras is considered a genius whose discoveries are still relevant. His theories became the basic foundation in mathematics and geometry and enabled further advances in architecture, design, construction, cartography, navigation, and astronomy. Pythagoras and his disciples discovered and applied the principles of harmonic oscillation, which are the basis for the intervals of vibrational tones. He is credited with introducing the seven-tone scale with mathematically determined ratios of vibrations on which Western music is based.

We enthusiastically utilized the talented Pythagoras in all areas. However, it was much more difficult for us to accept the basic message he was teaching and by which he acted—compassion for all living things and that it is our happiness depends on the loving treatment of animals. It also inspired Plato, Plutarch, Plotinus, the Gnostics, and early Christian priests. In 1850, the word vegetarian was coined. Until then anyone who did not eat meat was called a 'Pythagorean'.

The word "vegan" was coined in England in 1944 by Donald Watson. He was not satisfied with the word "vegetarian" because it did not take into account the motivation but only referred to the exclusion of animal meat from the diet. He took the first three and the last two letters of this word (English vegetarian). Today is the definition of veganism from the texts of the Vegan Association from England (Vegan Society), which says: "Veganism denotes a philosophy and a way of life that tends to exclude—as far as possible and practicable—all forms of exploitation and cruelty to animals for food, clothing or any other reason; in a broader sense, it promotes the development and use of alternatives that do not involve the use of animals, which benefit people, animals, and the environment."

Veganism highlights an ancient idea that has been debated for centuries, especially in spiritual movements around the world. It is a reflection of the longing for world peace, truth, justice, wisdom and freedom. It marks the birth of a new consciousness, the awakening of intelligence, compassion and intuition, and rejects cruelty and domination.

## What We Sow, We Reap

The horror we inflict on animals through exploitation for food, supported by the media and the food industry, is also increasing among humans.

As young animals are killed for food, suicide rates among children and teenagers increase. For example, we deliberately induce fear in laboratories where experiments are carried out on animals, as a result we find that fear also increases chronically in humans. When we force cows to overproduce milk and hens to overproduce eggs, we induce osteoporosis. While we humans get sick and suffer from the same diseases. We force animals into obesity, disease, overcrowding, anxiety, and stress, and we are becoming the same. We feed animals with food that is unnaturally grown and full of chemical additives.

Grocery stores sell "food" that is full of toxins and chemicals that fill our plates. When we restrict the movement of animals and lock them in cages, we notice, if we are honest, that we ourselves are confined in offices and other spaces where there is not much freedom of movement either. When we ignore the suffering of animals, we ignore our own suffering and the suffering of our fellow man.

It is an interesting fact that most people are disgusted by raw meat. Before eating it, it is always baked, boiled and seasoned to get an acceptable taste. We have to ask ourselves if we really enjoy the taste of meat, sausages, salami, pate. Additives mask and enhance the taste of animal products that we consume due to societal pressure and because we were raised that way.

Most types of cheese are made by boiling animal milk. Without salt and other additives, cheeses would be mostly tasteless. In order to make the products more palatable, cream, milk, fruit yogurt, and ice cream are added with various aromas, fruit, sugar, and other additives, the most controversial of which is carrageenan.

By exploiting animals for our purposes, we have ironically and inevitably created a system that exploits ourselves. Our net worth is measured in money, just like cows sell for kilograms.

Even vegan and vegetarian diets are not always the best choice. Modern vegans and vegetarians are exposed to many harmful substitutes sold by large corporations. Vegan steaks, sausages, hams, and cheeses also contain harmful additives to recreate a wide variety of tastes. Believe it or not, hummus, guacamole, and other spreads that can be bought in shopping centers and are labeled as "fresh" are not made from organic ingredients. The old story repeats itself in a modified form. If we choose not to eat meat, we do not need to buy meat substitutes. All necessary proteins can be obtained from cereals in combination with legumes. Some legumes even have more protein than meat or dairy products. Tofu, seitan, and tempeh can be prepared at home, as well as spreads and other substitutes.

The system we created ourselves forced us to have less and less time to prepare meals, that's why the fastest solution is to buy in a shopping center.

## The Number of Vegans Is Growing Among Athletes

I studied at a sports college, but I didn't finish it. Even though I "failed" as a student, sport was still the guiding principle in my life. The dynamics of my constitution drives me to constant movement, to various sports activities, especially to climbing and mountain climbing in recent years. The mountains give me the peace and quiet that I need so much.

I know quite a few top athletes who have already been flirting with a vegan or vegetarian diet for a long time. Years ago, I accompanied a friend, a mountain runner, on some of his races. His diet was mainly vegetarian. Before the race exclusively vegan. He won an enviable place as world champion in his category. This is a very big load for the organism, and such a result requires a lot of order, diet discipline and daily practice. Obviously, not everything in the much-vaunted proteins is of animal origin. Simon says it's all in the head.

Near the capital of Slovenia, Ljubljana, there is a hill called Šmarna gora. I often jump up in the morning to catch the sunrise. I often met Zdenka Mihelič, a mountain guide, vegan, and journalist for Planinski Vestnik. Planinski Vestnik is a Slovenian magazine for mountain climbers and everyone who loves the mountains. Once, when we were chasing the sunrise, we came up with the idea of organizing a vegan workshop for caretakers of Slovenian cabins in Erjavčeva's cabin in Vršič, located in the Julian Alps. I thought the idea was beautiful. Vegans and vegetarians do not have much choice when they come to the mountains to order something light and easy to digest. The menu usually includes meat, turnips, cabbage with sausage, stews with meat, or buckwheat with sour milk and crackers. This kind of food is heavy and stays in the stomach. Walking and climbing after such meals is tiring and difficult, as it is not pleasant to have pressure in the stomach. Those who do not eat meat always carry food with them.

**Fruits and Vegetables of Questionable Origin**

In the markets, vegetables and fruits are primarily of questionable origin and mainly integrated. Most vegetables and fruits come from Italy, Pordenone, and Spain, where very unhealthy products come from. It is not easy to find a farm that grows vegetables organically. It is like looking for a needle in a haystack. Only self-sustaining do we know for sure what we have on our plate. Those who live in the city and do not have this option will probably come forward. There is a solution for them too.

More and more self-sufficient farms and communities grow according to the principles of biodynamics or have permaculture gardens. They often need help, so we can take some of our free time and help them, or we can go there and present Seva (selfless service). Believe me; you will always leave with baskets full of healthy vegetables and fruits. So we are always in the sound and a smiling company of healthy people. Years ago, I visited such centers in Europe. I stopped at organic farms, where they needed help with farming. I have always been blessed with exceptional lunches made from organic vegetables and fruit, accommodation, and wonderful fellowship that included yoga, meditation, and Tai chi. Some of them did their best to reward me with a bit of money. I returned to Umbria, where I helped at the organic farm Santa Maria in San Venanzo to harvest more than 2,000 olives that have never been treated with chemicals. Near Genoa, more precisely above the town of Borzonasca, there is another magical place, a self-sufficient center—Centro Anidra. Eight years ago, when I was last time there, we planted many roses, the flowers of which are now used to make rose water and jam. The center also produces cosmetics, herbs, olive oil, and more.

Here in Slovenia, many people grow organically and form a community because the future lies in the association. As Dr. Tuttle says, the system divides us instead of connects us. As our intelligence declines, we become disconnected from a sense of service to larger groups, less sensitive to feedback from those groups, and increasingly selfish and self-reliant. This insensitivity is stupidity, which inevitably brings violence, disease, misfortune, wars, suffering and death.[43]

Where there is will and motivation, there is always the right path and solution.

# Endnotes

[1] https://www.brainyquote.com/quotes/albert_einstein
_138241

[2] https://twitter.com/_stoicteacher/status/16131589904
97685505

[3] slovenian version, Biologija prepričanj, dr. Bruce H.
Lipton, (The biology of belief) Založba Primus –
Brežice 2019

[4] *slovenian website:* Srečko Šorli,
https://sensa.metropolitan.si/osebna-rast/vrelec-
vecne-mladosti-in-biofotonska-prehrana
https://sensa.metropolitan.si/osebna-rast/clovek-
lahko-z-zavestjo-spremeni-svoj-genski-zapis/

[5] https://www.brainyquote.com/quotes/arthur_schopen
hauer_103608

[6] slovenian version, Biologija prepričanj, dr. Bruce H.
Lipton, (The biology of belief), Založba Primus –
Brežice 2019, page 67, 68, 69, 70, 71. (The Biology
of Belief 2005)

[7] slovenian version, Oprani možgani, Robert H.
Lustig, (The Hacking of the American Mind).

[8] slovenian version, Oprani možgani, Robert H. Lustig, The Hacking of the American Mind.

[9] https://www.azquotes.com/quote/843066

[10] I used slovenian version, Julijan Johnson, Pot mojstrov, 1994, (The Path of the Masters), page 371, 372

[11] https://www.heartmath.org/

[12] slovenian version, Julijan Johnson, Pot mojstrov, 1994, (The Path of the Masters),

[13] https://www.goodreads.com/quotes/83999-as-long-as-man-continues-to-be-the-ruthless-destroyer

[14] slovenian version, Esenska poslanica miru – Edmund Bordeaux Szekely, translated to slovenian language by dr. France Susman, (The Essene Gospel of Peace) page 3, 4, 5, 6,7, 11

[15] slovenian version, Esenska poslanica miru – Edmund Bordeaux Szekely, translated to slovenian language by dr. France Susman, (The Essene Gospel of Peace) page 12.

[16] http://www.preseren.net/slo/3_poezije/40_vzrok.asp France Prešeren (1800–1849) was the greatest Slovenian poet.

[17] slovenian version, Esenska poslanica miru – Edmund Bordeaux Szekely, translated to slovenian language by dr. France Susman, (The Essene Gospel of Peace) page 8

I used direct quotes.

[18] slovenian version, Esenska poslanica miru –
Edmund Bordeaux Szekely, translated to slovenian
language by dr. France Susman, (The Essene Gospel
of Peace) page 9

[19] slovenian version, Esenska poslanica miru –
Edmund Bordeaux Szekely, translated to slovenian
language by dr. France Susman, (The Essene Gospel
of Peace), page 23

[20] slovenian version, Esenska poslanica miru –
Edmund Bordeaux Szekely, translated to slovenian
language by dr. France Susman, (The Essene Gospel
of Peace), page 24,25

[21] I used slovenian version, Esenska poslanica miru –
Edmund Bordeaux Szekely, translated to slovenian
language by dr. France Susman, (The Essene Gospel
of Peace), page 37, 38, 39,

[22] I used slovenian version, Esenska poslanica miru –
Edmund Bordeaux Szekely, translated to slovenian
language by dr. France Susman, (The Essene Gospel
of Peace), page 40

[23]https://www.brainyquote.com/quotes/robert_louis_s
tevenson_163019

[24] slovenian version, (The end of food), Konec Hrane
– Paul Roberts, založba Učila International, 2009,
page 37, 38 – I used direct quotes from the book

<sup>25</sup> https://www.amazon.com/End-Food-Paul-
Roberts/dp/0547085974
slovenian version, (The end of food), Konec Hrane –
Paul Roberts, založba Učila International, 2009, page
40, 41, 42, 44, 46, 47 – I used direct quotes from the
book
<sup>26</sup> I used slovenian version, (The end of food), Konec
Hrane – Paul Roberts, založba Učila International,
2009, direct quotes
<sup>27</sup> slovenian version, (The end of food), Konec Hrane
– Paul Roberts, založba Učila International, 2009,
direct quotes
<sup>28</sup> I used slovenian version, (The end of food), Konec
Hrane – Paul Roberts, založba Učila International,
2009.
<sup>29</sup> slovenian version, (The end of food), Konec Hrane
– Paul Roberts, založba Učila International, 2009,
direct quotes
<sup>30</sup> slovenian version, Zdravi možgani, David
Perlmutter, UMco d.o.o. 2017 (Brain Maker) page 29.
I used direct quotes
<sup>31</sup> I used slovenian version, Zdravi možgani, David
Perlmutter, UMco d.o.o. 2017 (Brain Maker) page
117, 118. I used direct quotes from the book

[32] slovenian version, Zdravi možgani, David Perlmutter, UMco d.o.o. 2017 (Brain Maker) page 117, 118. I used direct quotes from the book

[33] https://www.sciencedirect.com/topics/medicine-and-dentistry/sirtuin-1

[34] https://www.sciencedirect.com/topics/medicine-and-dentistry/sirtuin-1

[35] https://www.tagoreweb.in/Verses/one-hundred-poems-of-kabir-202/o-sadhu!-purify-your-3899

[36] https://www.azquotes.com/quote/99147

[37] I used slovenian version, Ko telo reče ne, Gabor Mate, Založba Primus, Brežice 2018. (When the Body Says No), page 87

[38] slovenian version, Zdravi možgani, David Perlmutter, UMco d.o.o. 2017 (Brain Maker), page 100

[39] Boro Leban is a friend of mine and he wrote a song for me and it is not published anywhere. I added the year he wrote it.

[40] https://quotes.thefamouspeople.com/kabir-6814.php

[41] https://rudolfsteinerquotes.wordpress.com/tag/protein/

Source: Rudolf Steiner – GA 354 – The Evolution of the Earth and Man and The Influence of the Stars – Lecture VI – Dornach, 31st July, 1924

[42] https://www.humanedecisions.com/george-bernard-shaw-animals-are-my-friends-and-i-dont-eat-my-friends/

[43] I used slovenian version, Hrana za Mir, Will Tuttle, Ph.D., Založba Avrora d.o.o. 2013 (The world pice diet – 2004), page, 123, 124